BRIGHT NOTES

JULIUS CAESAR
BY
WILLIAM
SHAKESPEARE

Intelligent Education

INFLUENCE
PUBLISHERS

Nashville, Tennessee

BRIGHT NOTES: Julius Caesar
www.BrightNotes.com

No part of this publication may be used or reproduced in any manner whatsoever without written permission, except in the case of brief quotations in critical articles and reviews. For permissions, contact Influence Publishers http://www.influencepublishers.com.

ISBN: 978-1-645425-66-3 (Paperback)
ISBN: 978-1-645425-67-0 (eBook)

Published in accordance with the U.S. Copyright Office Orphan Works and Mass Digitization report of the register of copyrights, June 2015.

Originally published by Monarch Press.
Robert Jacob Littman; Frances K. Barasch; W John Campbell, 1964
2020 Edition published by Influence Publishers.

Interior design by Lapiz Digital Services. Cover Design by Thinkpen Designs.

Printed in the United States of America.

Library of Congress Cataloging-in-Publication Data forthcoming.
Names: Intelligent Education
Title: BRIGHT NOTES: Julius Caesar
Subject: STU004000 STUDY AIDS / Book Notes

CONTENTS

INTRODUCTION TO WILLIAM SHAKESPEARE

. . . .

On April 26, 1564, William Shakespeare, son of John Shakespeare and Mary Arden, was christened in Holy Trinity Church, Stratford-on-Avon. His birthday is traditionally placed three days before. He was the eldest of four boys and two girls born to his father, a well-to-do glover and trader, who also held some minor offices in the town government. He probably attended the local free school, where he picked up the "small Latin and less Greek" that Ben Jonson credits him with. ("Small" Latin to that knowledgeable classicist meant considerably more than it does today.) As far as is known, this was the extent of Shakespeare's formal education. In November of 1582, when he was eighteen, a license was issued for his marriage to Ann Hathaway, a Stratford neighbor eight years older than himself. The following May their child Susanna was christened in the same church as her father. While it may be inferred from this that his marriage was a forced one, such an inference is not necessary; engagement at that time was a legally binding contract and was sometimes construed as allowing conjugal rights. Their union produced two more children, twins Judith and Hamnet, christened in February, 1585. Shortly thereafter Shakespeare left Stratford for a career in London. What he did during these years - until we pick him up, an established playwright, in 1592 - we do not know, as no records exist. It is presumed that he served an apprenticeship in the theatre, perhaps as a provincial trouper, and eventually won himself a place as an actor. By 1594 he was a successful dramatist with the Lord Chamberlain's company (acting groups had noble protection and patronage), having produced the *Comedy of Errors* and the *Henry VI* trilogy, probably in collaboration with older, better established dramatists. When the plague closed the London theatres for many months of 1593-94, he found himself without a livelihood. He promptly turned his hand to poetry (although written in verse, plays were not considered as dignified as poetry), writing two long narrative poems, *Venus and Adonis* and *The Rape of Lucrece*. He dedicated them to the Earl of Southampton, undoubtedly receiving some recompense. The early nineties also saw the first of Shakespeare's **sonnets** circulating in manuscript, and later finding their way into print. In his early plays - mostly chronicle histories glorifying England's past, and light comedies - Shakespeare sought for popular success and achieved it. In 1599 he was able to buy a share in the Globe Theatre, where he acted and where his plays were performed. His ever-increasing financial success enabled him to buy a good deal of real estate in his native Stratford, and by 1605 he was able to retire from acting. Shortly thereafter he began to spend most of his time in Stratford, to which he retired around 1610. Very little is known of his life after he left London. He died on April 23, 1616, in Stratford, and was buried there. In 1623 the *First Folio* edition of his complete works was published by a group of his friends as a testimonial to his memory. This was a very rare tribute, because at the time plays were generally considered to be inferior literature, not really worthy of publication. These scanty facts, together with some information about the dates of his plays, are all that is definitely known about the greatest writer in the history of English literature. The age in which Shakespeare lived was not as concerned with keeping accurate records as we are, and any further details about Shakespeare's life have been derived from educated guesses based on knowledge of his time. Shakespeare's plays fall into three major groups according to the periods in his development when he wrote them:

EARLY COMEDIES AND HISTORIES

The first group consists of romantic comedies such as *A Midsummer Night's Dream* (1593-5), and of strongly patriotic histories such as *Henry V* (1599). The early comedies are full of farce and slapstick, as well as exuberant poetry. Their plots are complicated and generally revolve around a young love relationship. The histories are typical of the robust, adventurous English patriotism of the Elizabethan era, when England had achieved a position of world dominance and power.

THE GREAT TRAGEDIES

The second period, beginning with *Hamlet* and ending with *Antony and Cleopatra*, is the period of the great tragedies: *Hamlet* (1602); *Othello* (1604); *King Lear* (1605); *Macbeth* (1606); and *Antony and Cleopatra* (1607-8). Shakespeare seems to have gone through a mental crisis at this time. His vision of the world darkens, and he sees life as an **epic** battle between the forces of good and evil, between order and chaos within man and in the whole universe. The forces for good win out in the end over evil, which is self-defeating. But the victory of the good is at great cost and often comes at the point of death. It is a moral victory, not a material one. These tragedies center on a great man who, because of some flaw in his makeup, or some error he commits, brings death and destruction down upon himself and those around him. They are generally considered the greatest of Shakespeare's plays.

THE LATE ROMANCES

In the third period Shakespeare returns to romantic comedy. But such plays as *Cymbeline* (1609-10), *The Winter's Tale* (1610-11), and *The Tempest* (1611) are very different in point of view and structure from such earlier comedies as *Much Ado About Nothing* (1599) and *Twelfth Night* (1600). Each of these late romances has a situation potentially tragic, and there is much bitterness in them. Thus the destructive force of insane jealousy serves as the **theme** both of the tragedy, *Othello*, and the comedy, *The Winter's Tale*. They are serious comedies, replacing farce and slapstick with rich symbolism and supernatural events. They deal with such **themes** as sin and redemption, death and rebirth, and the conflict between nature and society, rather than with simple romantic love. In a sense they are deeply religious, although unconnected with any church dogma. In his last play, *The Tempest*, Shakespeare achieved a more or less serene outlook upon the world after the storm and stress of his great tragedies and the so-called "dark comedies."

SHAKESPEARE'S THEATRE

Shakespeare's plays were written for a stage very different from our own. Women, for instance, were not allowed to act; so female parts, even that of Cleopatra, were played by boy actors whose voices had not yet changed. The plays were performed on a long platform surrounded by a circular, unroofed theatre, and were dependent on natural daylight for lighting. There was no curtain separating the stage from the audience, nor were there act divisions. These were added to the plays by later editors. Because the stage jutted right into the audience, Shakespeare was able to achieve a greater intimacy with his spectators than modern playwrights can. The audience in the pit, immediately surrounding the stage, had to stand crowded together throughout the play. Its members tended to be lower class Londoners who would frequently comment aloud on the action of the play and break into fights. Anyone who attended the plays in the pit did so at the risk of having his pockets picked, of catching a disease, or, at best, of being jostled about by the crude "groundlings." The aristocratic and merchant classes, who watched the plays from seats in the galleries, were spared most of the physical discomforts of the pit.

ITS ADVANTAGES

There were certain advantages, however, to such a theatre. Because complicated scenic, lighting and sound effects were impossible, the playwright had to rely on the power of his words to create scenes in the audience's imagination. The rapid changes of scene and vast distances involved in *Antony and Cleopatra*, for instance, although they create a problem for modern producers, did not for Shakespeare. Shakespeare did not rely - as the modern realistic theatre does - on elaborate stage scenery to create atmosphere and locale. For these, as for battle scenes involving large numbers of people, Shakespeare relied on the suggestive power of his poetry to quicken the imagination of his audience. Elizabethan audiences were very lively anyway, and quick to catch any kind of word play. Puns, jokes, and subtle poetic effects made a greater impression on them than on modern audiences, who are less alert to language.

INTRODUCTION TO JULIUS CAESAR

. . . .

BRIEF SUMMARY OF JULIUS CAESAR

As the play opens, the Roman people have turned out to celebrate the triumphal return of Caesar from his victory over Pompey (a member of the first triumvirate and champion of the Republic). Flavius and Marullus, two tribunes (officers appointed to protect the interests of the people from possible injustice at the hands of patrician magistrates) disperse the crowd of commoners, arguing that Caesar's triumph in civil war is no cause for celebration and that the people had much better weep for Pompey, who they had formerly adored.

Accompanied by fanfare and a large following, Caesar arrives to witness the race traditionally held on the Feast of Lupercal, which is being celebrated on the same day. A soothsayer warns Caesar to beware the ides of March, but Caesar peruses the man's face and dismisses him as a dreamer. Meanwhile, Cassius tell Brutus of his resentment of Caesar's growing power. As Caesar emerges from the race, he eyes Cassius and tells Antony that he does not trust men with a lean and hungry look. Casca joins Brutus and Cassius and describes how Caesar has reluctantly refused the crown offered to him three times by Mark Antony. Brutus promises to think over Cassius's fear that Caesar's ambition is a danger to the democracy of Rome and agrees to meet him the next day. Casca is invited to join them.

During a violent storm, Casca and Cicero meet and discuss the great wonders that have occurred that night. After Cicero leaves, Cassius arrives, explains the omens of the storm and discusses a conspiracy against Caesar. They both plot how they might win Brutus over to their side completely, for he is already inclined against Caesar.

Alone in his garden, Brutus debates with himself over the threat that Caesar poses to the Republic. At last he decides that Caesar must be killed because he might become a tyrant. The conspirators, Cassius, Casca, Decius, Brutus, Cinna, Metellus Cimber, and Trebonius arrive at this point, and Brutus sanctions the decision to kill Caesar the next day when he is to receive the crown of king. They decide that only Caesar is to die. Portia, Brutus' wife, enters after the conspirators have left. She entreats Brutus to tell her what is happening, but as he is about to reveal the conspiracy to her, another conspirator, Ligarius, arrives and takes Brutus away.

Caesar, meanwhile, spends a restless night. His wife, Calpurnia, begs him not to go to the Senate meeting that day because she has dreamed that she saw a statue of him, spouting blood like a fountain, and because of the ominous events which have occurred during the storm. Caesar sends his servant to the seers to make a sacrifice and to determine what the gods are trying to say. The augurers tell Caesar to stay at home, and Caesar decides to comply, especially since his wife has urged him so strongly. However, one of the conspirators, Caesar's good friend, Decius Brutus, persuades him to go to the Senate by pointing out how ridiculous he would seem to heed his wife's superstitions.

The same morning, Artemidorus, a teacher of rhetoric, prepares a letter for Caesar, warning him of the conspiracy. The Soothsayer also prepares to stop Caesar outside the Capitol to warn him of harm, and Portia, who now knows Brutus' plan, anxiously anticipates its outcome.

Caesar is given two warnings; he ignores them both, goes into the Senate, and after a speech in which he arrogantly praises himself, he is stabbed by the conspirators.

Mark Antony, who has been lured out of the Senate by Trebonius, returns after the murder and pretends to join the conspirators. When left alone with the body of Caesar, however, Antony vows to avenge the murder, even if he has to throw all Italy into civil war to do it. Meanwhile, Octavius, Caesar's heir, arrives near Rome. Antony and a servant carry Caesar's body out to the Forum. Brutus addresses the crowd first, telling them that Caesar was killed because he was too ambitious. The crowd reacts favorably to Brutus and is ready to make him a second Caesar, but Brutus orders them to listen to Antony's funeral oration for Caesar.

In a brilliantly ironic speech, Antony inflames the crowd against the conspirators. The crowd runs wildly through the streets, determined to burn the houses of the conspirators. The mob comes upon Cinna the poet who happens to have the same name as one of the conspirators, and for the sake of destruction, they tear him to pieces. Brutus and Cassius flee from Rome. Antony, Octavius, and Lepidus unite forces, calling themselves the second triumvirate. They prepare to put to death those whom they suspect will be hostile to their cause.

Brutus and Cassius, meanwhile, have gathered their forces in Sardis in Asia Minor. Their destruction is forecast when the

Turkey

Republican leaders begin to quarrel with each other. Brutus rebukes Cassius because the latter has permitted an officer to take bribes and because he has not been sending money to Brutus, who has ben unable to raise his own funds. His anger spent, Brutus apologizes for his ill-temper and informs Cassius that Portia has killed herself. By the time official word is brought that Portia is dead, Brutus accepted the news with quiet resignation. During the night, Brutus sees the ghost of Caesar, who says that they will meet again at Philippi.

Cassius and Bruius then march to Philippi in Greece to meet the armies of Antony and Octavius. The generals meet and exchange insults before the battle begins. In the first engagement, Antony overcomes Cassius, while Brutus overcomes Octavius' wing. Cassius retires to a nearby hill, and when he mistakes approaching horsemen for enemies, he runs upon a sword held by his servant, Pindarus. Brutus and not the enemy arrives, finds Cassius' body, and sends it away for burial. There is another skirmish and Brutus' forces are defeated completely. Unwilling to endure the dishonor of capture, Brutus commits suicide with the aid of his servant, Strato. Antony and Octavius find Brutus' body, over which Antony states, "This was the noblest Roman of them all." Octavius declares that Brutus will receive burial befitting his virtue, and calls an end to battle as the play concludes.

JULIUS CAESAR

. . . .

ACT I: SCENE I

The play opens in a street in Rome. Two tribunes, Flavius and Marullus, are dispersing the crowds that have gathered there. The tribunes have trouble extracting an explanation from a cobbler who appears to be leading the mob, for the cobbler gives equivocal answers to the direct questions of the officials. He claims to be a "mender of bad soles," "a surgeon to old shoes," and one who lives by the "awl." Finally, he admits that the workingmen have left their shops and have assembled "to see Caesar and to rejoice in his triumph."

Comment

Although the scene is Rome, the atmosphere is Elizabethan, and the workers here behave like pert Tudor craftsmen. In his portrayal of crowds and of workingmen, Shakespeare frequently relied on humor to establish the unruly atmosphere and vulgar tone of the scene. The cobbler's humor is typical of his craft, and he puns on the words of his trade: "all" (awl), "cobbler" (shoemaker, bungler), "sole," (soul), "out" (out of shoes, out of temper), "recover" (save, mend).

Elizabethan trades were ranked according to the dignity of the craft, and although the shoemaker's trade was among the lowest, Shakespeare has the cobbler lead the mob, partly to show how vulgar the leadership is, and partly because of the popular legend of the shoemaker who became the leader of the people and the mayor of London.

Flavius and Marullus are Tribunes of the People, officers who were appointed to protect the interests of plebeians from injustices that might be perpetrated by patrician magistrates. They could reverse a magistrate's judgment or inflict punishment on a plebeian. In Caesar's time, however, their powers were nominal. In this scene, the tribunes are trying to protect the democracy of Rome by preventing their charges from installing a dictator in office.

Marullus is incensed by the reason he is given. He rebukes the commoners for gathering to honor Caesar. What territories has Caesar conquered for Rome, the tribune asks; what prisoners has he led home? He reproaches the people for their hard hearts and senseless cruelty in forgetting Pompey so soon after they had cheered him. He reminds the mob of how they had lined the streets and climbed the battlements of buildings, sitting there all day with babes in arms to get just a glimpse of Pompey when he returned after a victory. "And do you now strew flowers in his way/ That comes in triumph over Pompey's blood?" Marullus harangues. He warns the unfeeling mob that their ingratitude will be repaid by plague if they do not disperse immediately and pray mercy of the gods. Flavius enjoins the people to run to the

Tiber and weep for Pompey until the river is filled with tears up to its highest bank.

Comment

The tribunes' harangues are spoken from the point of view of the Republican who is sickened by the conquest of a Roman over a Roman. Caesar's triumph was not over a foreign nation but over Pompey and his sons, all fellow Romans. Pompey had been a member of the first triumvirate, formed in 60 B.C. by Pompey, Caesar, and Crassus. They were a coalition group, holding supreme political authority over Rome, subject to the advice and veto of the Senate, a legislative body, comprised mainly of noblemen or patricians. Pompey was married to Caesar's daughter by a former wife, but after the daughter's death, disagreement flared out between Caesar and Pompey. As champion for the Senate, Pompey fought Caesar when he sought to overthrow the triumvirate, disobey the Senate, and establish himself as dictator of Rome. Pompey was assassinated in Egypt, but his sons continued his fight at Munda in Spain. The death of Pompey's sons, that is "Pompey's blood," meant the death of the Republic, for which the plebeians should have no cause to rejoice.

The commoners, however, are more concerned with personal favors than with abstract political principles and the interests of the mainly patrician Senate. They have been won over to Caesar's side by his previous gifts to the people. After his triumph of 46 B.C., for example, Caesar entertained the people with feasts and shows and gave one hundred denarii to each citizen. The capricious nature of the mob is established at this point when Marullus complains about their ingratitude and the fickle transfer of their affections from Pompey, whom they had formerly adored, to Caesar.

When the commoners leave, Flavius remarks, "They vanish tongue-tied in their guiltiness." Then he instructs Marullus to go through the city and "disrobe the images," that is, remove the decorations intended to honor Caesar. Marullus asks if it would not be sacrilege to remove the decorations for the Feast of Lupercal, which is being celebrated on this same day, but Flavius replies that it does not matter. He also orders Marullus to drive the vulgar from the streets so that the absence of the people (who grew like feathers on Caesar's wing and enable him to fly higher than he otherwise could) will keep Caesar's ambitions in check.

Comment

The idea of desecration is suggested at this point in connection with the removal of the decorations for Caesar's triumph and the Feast of Lupercal. The Lupercalia was an annual festival, celebrated in honor of the god Pan or Faunus and administered by the members of two ancient families of Rome. In 44 B.C., the Luperci Iulii was instituted in honor of Julius Caesar, which probably explains why Shakespeare condensed history so that Caesar's triumph and the Lupercalia would fall on the same day.

The purpose of the feast held in February was to secure expiation, purification, and fertility for the spring planting. The rites included a race around the Palatine by two youths carrying thongs made from a sacrificed he-goat. Women who stood in the path of the runners would receive blows from the thongs, which were believed to be a charm against barrenness.

Shakespeare achieved special effects by telescoping history. In this scene, he makes Caesar's return coincide with the Lupercalia, suggesting thereby that Caesar, the astute politician, had timed his arrival for a day on which the streets would be crowded with a cheerful public and the statues adorned for the feast as well as for his return. In this way, objections that the people were not at work or that the statues were adorned in his honor would be answered by the feast. At the same time, Caesar would be associating his return with a religious occasion and work on the superstitions of the people who would eventually proclaim him a god and accept him as their dictator. It was in this month, in fact, that Caesar was proclaimed Dictator Perpetuus (dictator for life) and that the Lupercalia was named in his honor.

The idea of Caesar's ambition is introduced in Flavius' **metaphor** of the bird, in which he states that the people's adulation allows Caesar to place himself above other citizens of the Republic and that there is danger he will become a king and keep "us all in servile fearfulness."

SUMMARY

This first scene works as a skillful introduction to the major action of the play. It represents the crowd as a vulgar and capricious mob, who will be important in the political action which ensues. It supplies the background of events to come by representing the civil disorder which exists in Rome and the differences which exist between two main factions of the city; the commoners who favor Caesar and the tribunes who are Republicans. The case for the Republicans is stated by Marullus, who is angry at the "senseless" mob for celebrating Caesar's triumph over Pompey, another Roman. Flavius establishes the fact that Caesar is ambitious, that he flies too high, and that he is a danger to free men. It is suggested that Caesar is a shrewd politician for arranging his arrival to coincide with the Feast of Lupercal, when crowds would be available to cheer him and when images would be adorned to honor him as well as the god Faunus. The idea of desecration is suggested when Flavius orders the disrobing of the images.

ACT I: SCENE II

Shortly after the crowds have been dispersed by the tribunes, a procession arrives. There is music and pageantry as Caesar, Antony, Calpurnia, Portia, Decius, Brutus, Cicero, Brutus, Cassius, and Casca, dressed in elegant attire, march through the street. A large crowd follows the procession which is on its way to the race traditionally held on the Lupercal.

Caesar calls to his wife, Calpurnia, and tells her to stand directly in Antony's way, as he runs through the streets. He orders Antony to strike her since "the barren touched in this holy chase, /Shake off their sterile curse." Antony replies to Caesar's command, "When Caesar says 'do this,' it is performed."

Comment

At the Feast of Lupercal, young noblemen ran naked through the streets, striking women, who deliberately stood in their way, believing that if they were pregnant, they should deliver well, and if they were barren, that they would become pregnant. Antony's comment shows that he is Caesar's devoted and obedient follower.

From the crowd a Soothsayer emerges and cries to Caesar, "Beware the ides of March!" Caesar asks the Soothsayer to come forward and repeat what he has just said. He peruses the man's face, hears the warning again, and decides, "He is a dreamer; let us leave him."

Comment

The Soothsayer's prophetic warning is heavy with dramatic **irony**, for the audience knows that Caesar will be killed on the ides (the fifteenth) of March, while Caesar, who studies the man and his words, exercises poor judgment in dismissing both.

In ancient Greek drama, the solution of an oracle or riddle brought about the tragic resolution of the play at the point when the hero learned the true meaning of the oracle. The ambiguous prophecy of the Soothsayer works in a similar way. It creates dramatic suspense as the audience anticipates Caesar's discovery of the tragic import of the riddle.

As Caesar and his followers go off to the feast, Cassius and Brutus remain behind. Brutus tells Cassius that he will not follow the course of the young men (as they race around the city), for he is not "game-some" and has not Antony's "quick spirit." Cassius expresses his fear that his good friend Brutus disapproves of him, for his looks no longer show his former love. Brutus assures Cassius that he is not vexed with his friend but with himself. He is, in fact, "with himself at war" and "forgets the show of love to other men."

Comment

The friendship and love between Brutus and Cassius is established in this conversation, and indication is given for the first time that Brutus is in a state of inner conflict. The face as a reflection of the feelings and thoughts of men is a recurrent **theme** in this scene. Caesar has scanned the soothsayer's face and has misjudged him as a dreamer, and Cassius has misjudged Brutus' "ungentle" eyes as a sign of his own disfavor.

Next, Cassius will read Brutus' face to him as if he were holding up a mirror before him. The mirror as a reflection of the moral nature of man was a popular device in the literature of Tudor England. The book called *A Mirror for Magistrates*, consisting of a series of morally edifying biographies of famous princes, went through eight editions in the years between 1555 and 1587. Its **theme**, copied by such notable writers as George Gascoigne, Samuel Daniel, and Michael Drayton, had a powerful influence on the chronicle plays of the 1580s and 1590s, Shakespeare's included. The idea was to present stories or biographies of important men who, through some flaw of character, worked out their destinies in a tragic way. The retelling of these tragedies was expected to have a moral influence on the reader.

In addition, poems like Gascoigne's *Steel Glass* and Sir John Davies' *Nosce Teipsum* used the mirror device as a means of reflecting the abuses of the times and the horrors of man's own sinful nature. It was important for man to learn to "know thyself," these poems taught; man was to search his own nature for the causes of evil. Cassius' desire to show Brutus his reflection in other men's eyes has a Machiavellian cast to it. He wishes to influence him to join a conspiracy. Morally speaking, Brutus must discover his own nature by himself.

The various characters who participate in this scene are also described as reflections in other men's eyes, and it should be noted that Shakespeare unites dramatic **exposition**, characterization, and dialogue through the use of the mirror metaphor.

Relieved to learn that he is still in Brutus' favor, Cassius tells his friend that he had misunderstood his emotional state and had refrained from discussing important matters with him. He asks Brutus if he can read his own character, which shines in his own face, revealing that Brutus is a just man. Many men, "except immortal Caesar," are now enslaved by Caesar's rule and wish that Brutus had Caesar's eyes so that Brutus could see his own nobility as Caesar sees his own.

Comment

Cassius has uttered the first in a series of persuasive remarks designed to win Brutus to the anti-Caesarsist cause. His reference to "immortal Caesar" is a sarcastic and covert **allusion** to the dictator's wish to be declared a god and to his ambitious desire to rise above his fellow Romans, who consider themselves his equals. Brutus is self-effacing, apparently, and Cassius works on his natural humility by reporting the praise other men have give, him. At the same time, he is suggesting that many respected men of Rome compare Brutus to Caesar, wishing that Brutus had a higher opinion of himself so that he might take action against the self-esteeming dictator. Thus, the characters of Brutus and Caesar are juxtaposed from the conspirator's point of view; Brutus' humility is contrasted with Caesar's presumptuousness and arrogance.

Having thus complimented Brutus, Cassius prepares to tell Brutus the subject of his argument. But first, he testifies to his own honest character, his veracity, his sobriety, his loyalty to friends.

Comment

Cassius is following rhetorical procedure in the persuasive argument he is about to deliver. He fails to come straight to the point, but first greets and compliments his audience, then attempts to establish the authority of the speaker. (Brutus will use this device in his address to the mob after Caesar's death.) Cassius' oratory is cut short, however, when a fanfare is sounded from the market-place, but after the interruption, Cassius announces his subject and proceeds to develop it.

Shouts are heard and a sennet is sounded (a series of bars played on a trumpet, symbolizing sovereignty). Brutus blurts out his fear that the people have chosen Caesar for their king. Cassius latches on to Brutus' expression of fear: "Ay do you fear it"/ Then must I think you would not have it so." Briefly, Brutus answers that he would not have Caesar king, and yet he loves him. Then he urges Cassius to go on with his message and promises that if it concerns the general good, even the fear of death will not permit him from doing what is honorable.

Comment

Caught unaware, Brutus states his inner conflict between his duty to the Republic and his personal love for Caesar. He admits, however, that he loves honor more than he fears death, and that he will act in the public good at any cost. Cassius' course is now clear to him. He must convince Brutus that the removal of Caesar is in the public interest.

Elizabethans associated the ancient Romans with the idea of noble friendship and dedicated statesmanship. Shakespeare expected his audience to realize the deep perturbation which would arise in a man when these two ideals came into conflict.

Returning to his speech and taking his cue from Brutus' remark about honor, Cassius announces his subject is honor. He cannot tell what other men think, but speaking for himself, Cassius states his preference for death to subjugation under a man who is no better than he. Caesar is just another such man, Cassius argues. He and Caesar were born equally free, were nurtured equally and endure the cold in the same way. In fact, Cassius claims, Caesar cannot swim as well as he, for once in a swimming contest, Cassius, like Aeneas (founder of Rome, who bore his father Anchises on his shoulders to save him from the flaming city of Troy), bore Caesar to safety on his shoulders. Another time, when Caesar was afflicted by fever in Spain, he cried for water as a sick girl might. Cassius is angered at the thought that a man of such "feeble temper" should now rule the majestic world alone, while Cassius, his equal, must bend to Caesar's slightest nod.

Comment

Cassius' reasons for hating Caesar are all personal ones and are, therefore, considered ignoble and envious. Cassius has indicated, however, that other noble Romans prefer death to slavery, although he does not pretend to be able to advance their motives. The portrait of Caesar is painted from a Republican's point of view, it should be remembered. Cassius emphasizes the physical deterioration, which Caesar actually displayed in the declining years of his life, but he ignores the heroic parts of the conquering hero. Cassius' amazement at Caesar's success reveals his own blindness to an important point. It is not Caesar's physical strength which has made him a dictator, but the spirit of Caesar, an intangible idea, which has raised him above his fellows.

The crowd roars and the trumpet flourishes a second time. Brutus surmises that some new honors are being heaped on Caesar. Cassius compares Caesar to a Colossus and calls Brutus and himself "petty men," who walk under the legs of this giant. "The fault, dear Brutus, is not in our stars,/ But in ourselves, that we are underlings," Cassius states. Then he asks: "Why should that name be sounded more than yours." Once more he alludes to Caesar's physical attributes and asks by what virtue he has become great: "Upon what meat doth this our Caesar feed/ That he is grown so great?" The reputation of Rome rests in the fact that it does not esteem "one only man." He ends his exhortation to Brutus by reminding him of his namesake, Lucius Junius Brutus (a Roman hero who had expelled Rome's last king, Tarquin, five hundred years earlier).

Comment

Cassius' reference to Brutus' namesake links Brutus with the ideal of liberty and the Republic. Cassius shows that he is concerned with the reputation of Rome and that he does not want Caesar's position for himself when he argues that "since the great flood" Rome "was famed with more than with one man." It has been argued, however, that Cassius is motivated solely by the desire for personal power and envy of Caesar. Antony says this too in the closing scene of the play. We should view Cassius, however, not as a black or white figure, but as a gray one, who is noble, although not the "noblest."

Brutus replies to Cassius' argument point for point. He assures Cassius that he is not suspicious of his love and that he is somewhat inclined toward Cassius' sentiments. But exactly what he thinks of conditions in Rome must be discussed at another time. Brutus promises to consider what Cassius has already said, to listen to him further and to answer him at a later time. For the present, Brutus tells Cassius, "chew upon this: "Brutus had rather be a villager/ Than to repute himself a son of Rome/ Under these hard conditions as this time/ Is like to lay upon us."

Comment

The "villager" to whom Brutus refers was neither a patrician nor a plebeian and not have rights as a citizen of Rome, but Brutus rhetorically asserts that even the villager's position is preferable to a Roman's under a monarchy. Brutus is not easily persuaded or inflamed by Cassius' passions. He shares Cassius' sentiments but has not yet decided if action is called for. Cassius, we shall see, is aware of Brutus' reflective nature and will use means other than argument to win Brutus to his cause.

The conversation is concluded by Caesar's return from the race. Brutus detects anger on the face of the dictator; he notices the paleness of Calpurnia's cheeks and the fires that burn from Cicero's eyes as if he had been "crossed in conference by some senators." Caesar, on his part, spies Cassius standing by, and turning to Antony, he tells him that he trusts fat men above lean ones. "Yond Cassius has a lean and hungry look!/ He thinks too much, such men are dangerous." Antony urges Caesar not to fear Cassius, for he is a noble Roman of excellent disposition. Caesar asserts that he has no fear, "for always I am Caesar," but if he had, he would avoid Cassius more than any other man. He contrasts Cassius with Antony, who loves plays and music and laughter. Cassius, on the other hand, is never entertained; he reads a great deal, watches men, and penetrates the motives behind their deeds. He rarely smiles, except as if in self-mockery. Such men are dangerous, Caesar warns Antony, insisting that he says this by way of instructing Antony in the ways of men and not because he is expressing his own fear. As Caesar leaves with his train, he bids Antony come to his right side, because he is deaf in the left ear, and tell him what he really thinks of Cassius.

Comment

The reading of faces is continued in this **episode**, and the respective observers interpret character from the appearance and habits of the man in question. Brutus observes the spot of anger on Caesar's brow and remarks that the whole company looks like a "chidden train." He deduces that something has happened which they do not like. Caesar characterizes Cassius as dangerous because he is observant and perceptive, traits which are appropriate to Cassius' lean and hungry look. Antony is apparently fatter, loves pleasure more than Cassius and values the noble arts of poetry and music; as a follower, Caesar implies, he is a man to be trusted.

This is the second of Caesar's brief appearances onstage since the opening of the play. Much has been said about him from the Republican point of view. The tribunes and Cassius fear Caesar's ambition, and Brutus indicates that he has similar trepidations himself. Apart from Caesar's costume and the pomp and ceremony which accompany his appearance, Caesar so far displays none of the special virtues which have made him a conqueror and dictator and beloved by the common people of Rome. His physical condition is in a state of decay. In his first appearance we learned that his wife is sterile, which suggests Caesar's own aging impotence. Now we see that he is deaf in one ear. According to dramatic chronology and Cassius' report, Caesar has recently suffered from fever in Spain and that he has never been especially adept in physical feats. Disease and infirmity will continue to be associated with Caesar until his tragic death scene. These infirmities reflect the diseases of his times; factionalism, civil disorder, and sacrilege, which finally overcome Caesar, but not his spirit, which lives on in Octavius. (Compare Caesar's infirmities with those of the king in Shakespeare's 2 *Henry IV*.)

Also worthy of notice is Caesar's protestation that he does not fear Cassius, "for always I am Caesar." This has been interpreted as a cover for Caesar's real fear of Cassius, as a sign of Caesar's arrogance for disdaining the emotions which other men have, and also as a mark of real fearlessness which is associated with the regal and courageous nature of the man.

When Caesar leaves, Brutus grasps Casca's cloak and asks the cause of Caesar's anger. Casca replies that Antony had offered him the crown three times and that three times Caesar refused it. Each time Antony held out the crown, Caesar fingered it, but discerning the mood of the mob which rejected monarchy, he put it aside. To Casca's thinking, however, he refused the crown more reluctantly each time. Then, Casca relates, Caesar fainted. Brutus remarks that Caesar has the falling-sickness (epilepsy). Cassius ironically replies that it is not Caesar, but they, who have the falling-sickness (that is, the Republic is falling). Having thrice refused the crown and thrice seen how glad the people were at his refusal, Casca continues, Caesar opened his doublet and offered them his throat to cut. Casca admits that if he had had a weapon, he would have taken up Caesar's offer. Casca goes on to say that when Caesar recovered from his fainting spell, he blamed his actions on his infirmity, and the mob forgave him. Casca ends his description with the words: "If Caesar had stabbed their mothers, they would have done no less."

Comment

We learn shortly that Casca is a "blunt fellow," who had a "quick mettle" (a good wit) at one time and which he still has when noble action calls for it. However, he has learned to put on "tardy form" (to act like a fool) and to appear to be rude in order to add "sauce" to "his good wit" so that men can better receive the truth he utters. Casca himself calls the business at the race "foolery," and so it was, according to Plutarch, who was Caesar's biographer. Like Plutarch, Casca suggests that Antony's offer of the crown and Caesar's refusal was a prearranged plan, designed to test the reactions of the crowd toward the elevation of Caesar from dictator to monarch. The crowd loves Caesar as dictator, but it is not ready to install him as monarch. The disappointment at having been cheered for refusing the crown explains Caesar's anger as he leaves the race.

Casca is a Republican, however, and he later joins the conspirators against Caesar. His interpretations of Caesar's refusal of the crown, as Casca repeatedly insists, is "to my thinking," "to my thinking," "and for mine own part." Shakespeare emphasizes that the description of events is being given from Casca's points of view and suggests that Caesar is more noble than Casca (or Plutarch) believes.

Casca's report and opinion roughly follows that of Plutarch's in his treatment of the **episode** in which Caesar offers his throat to be cut. In Plutarch, there is no doubt that Caesar wanted the crown and that he used ruses to test the people's reactions to his ambition. But in Shakespeare, the description of events is put into the mouth of a fool (who may not be a fool), and the entire subject of Caesar's ambition is thus put open to question. Was he ambitious, as Brutus later states, or did he put by the crown sincerely, as Antony implies.

In reply to Brutus' question on Cicero's reaction to the events at the Lupercalia, Casca answers that Cicero spoke Greek to his friends, but "it was Greek to me." He states further that Marullus and Flavius have been "silenced" for pulling garlands off Caesar's statues.

Comment

We learn that the images disrobed by the tribunes were really statues of Caesar bedecked with scarves of honor. The suggestion is that Caesar has allowed the people to treat him as a deity and that he has punished the tribunes for attempting to prevent their action. There is no doubt from Casca's point of view that Caesar is ambitious and presumptuous.

Seeing that Casca feels the same way toward Caesar as he does, Cassius invites him to dinner. After Casca leaves, Brutus comments that Casca is unpolished, but Cassius explains that Casca's rudeness is a mask behind which he can speak the truth freely. Repeating his promise to talk more the next day, Brutus leaves.

Alone on the stage, Cassius states that Brutus is a noble man, but that he sees Brutus can be diverted from his natural inclinations. Reflecting that noble minds should always keep company with other noble minds lest they be seduced, Cassius also observes that no one is so firm that he cannot be persuaded to change his course. He acknowledges that he is in Caesar's disfavor and that Brutus is loved by Caesar, but if he were Brutus, Cassius asserts, he would not let Caesar's love prevent him from following his principles. Cassius then announces his plan to win over Brutus completely. He will forge letters from leading citizens in which he will praise Brutus' name and hint covertly at Caesar's dangerous ambition to overthrow the Republic. After the letters have been thrown into Brutus' window and he has read them, Caesar should beware, for "We will shake him or worse days endure."

Comment

Cassius speaks the play's first soliloquy, a monologue in which the speaker reveals his thoughts to the audience. Since no dramatic interaction takes place during the soliloquy, it is a traditional dramatic **convention** that the speaker always utters the truth.

We learn Cassius' real feelings, motives, and plans from this speech. Brutus is indeed noble, but he can be moved. Cassius' reflection on the company noble minds should keep may mean that Brutus has made a mistake in befriending him, but it is more likely that Cassius feels Brutus is lucky to have him as a friend, for Cassius will lead him to "noble enterprise" (of the sort Casca will also participate in).

Cassius reveals, however, that he is capable of using devious means to achieve his "noble" end, the suppression of tyranny, but he raises the question, just how noble is that enterprise? Cassius is being portrayed as a careful and deceitful conspirator. As a lean and hungry man, he has already been identified as a Machiavellian type, whose cold statesmanship knows expediency, not honor. This was the common Elizabethan view of Machiavelli, author of *The Prince*, a book in the tradition of mirror-of-princes literature, which was extremely popular in the latter decades of the Tudor dynasty. The intellectual spirit of Machiavelli's book, however, did not reflect the moral teachings of English works in the same tradition. Machiavelli rejected metaphysics, theology, and idealism, and emphasized the necessity of political **realism** if the prince was to achieve and maintain his power. Deception, lies, and forgeries were all part of the Elizabethan conception of Machiavelli's statesmanship, and this conception is precisely what Cassius is meant to convey at this point. His cause may be honorable, but since his methods are not, he dishonors his cause. Cassius, however, will not always be seen as the practical, shrewd opportunist who would betray his friend (Caesar) if he were loved by him, for his character changes as the play progresses, and he commits suicide at the end, partly because he believes "his best friend" has been captured.

SUMMARY

Scene ii develops the political conflict already introduced in the first scene between the commoners who love Caesar and the tribunes who fear for the safety of the Republic. The mob and tribunes manifest the state of conflict in Rome on the plebeian level. Cassius, Brutus, and Caesar, in Scene ii, display political factionalism on the patrician level.

The major characters of the play are introduced in this scene, and their dispositions are examined from varying points of view. Caesar is seen amid all his pomp as a man concerned with religious ritual, the sterility of his wife, and the envious looks of Cassius. He shows his failing powers of perception when he dismisses the Soothsayer; he insists that he knows no fear; and he shows his wisdom of men and manners when he correctly diagnoses Cassius as a dangerous man. However, he admits to infirmity when he tells Antony to avoid his deaf ear and speak into his good one, and he suggests a growing hesitation in his own judgment when he asks Antony to give him his opinions of Cassius.

Antony, a member of Caesar's train, is a "gamesome" fellow who runs in the race of the Lupercal. He is unlike Brutus who has no inclination to participate in popular festivities, and he is opposite Cassius in that Antony is not lean and enjoys plays, music, and laughter. Caesar implies he is a loyal fellow, which he is indeed.

Cassius' character is opposed both to Antony's and Brutus'. He reads a great deal, fails to participate in entertainments, stands apart watching and thinking, and rarely laughs. He is a jealous man, uneasy at seeing another in power. He is a man to be feared. Cassius, moreover, is admittedly capable of betraying those who love him for the sake of his particular principles. He would use dishonorable means to achieve ends which he judges to be honorable.

Brutus' noble character is established by both Cassius and Caesar. Brutus is a reflective man, dedicated to the principles of the Republic, to love and friendship, to duty, and to honor. For the sake of honor, he will even face death (as, in fact, he does at the end of the play). But as strongly as he holds his ideals, he is just as strongly torn by conflicting loyalties to those ideals. Brutus makes decisions deliberately, and he is not quickly influenced by persuasive and passionate argument. He is torn between his love for Caesar and the anti-Caesar sentiments he admittedly shares with Cassius.

Casca has a rude manner and saucy wit, which he uses to disguise his satirical commentary on political events. He does not sympathize with Caesar and tends to interpret Caesar's behavior in the worst possible light. As a result of his denigrating interpretations of Caesar's ambition, he is invited to join the conspiratorial meeting which Cassius is planning.

Cicero is seen but not heard. He has a fiery look in his eye of the sort he has been known to show when arguing with senators. It is reported by Casca that he spoke Greek to the commoners who (since Casca cannot understand Greek) were not expected to understand Cicero. Those who did comprehend Cicero's Greek simply smiled at one another and shook their heads. Casca's implication is that Cicero is a pedant, who does not choose to speak in the language of the people.

Shakespeare foreshadows Caesar's assassination through the prophecy of the soothsayer and in the dialogue among Brutus, Cassius, and Casca. Thus, this scene lays the foundation for the conflicts, characterizations, and tragedy which will be developed throughout the play.

ACT I: SCENE III

It is the eve of the ides of March. Lightning flashes through the sky and thunder roars. On a street in Rome, Casca is seen with drawn sword, frightened out of his wits by the storm. He meets Cicero on the street and tells him that either there is "civil strife in heaven" or else men have offended the gods. He then describes other prodigies he has seen that night. A common slave's left hand was burned with flame, yet remained unscorched; a lion roamed loose near the Capitol; a hundred women have sworn they saw men walk in fire up and down the streets, and the birds of the night hooted and shrieked at noonday. Cicero philosophically replies, "Indeed, it is a strange-disposed time," but men interpret things absolutely contrary to the meaning of the events themselves. He asks Casca if Caesar is coming to the Capitol tomorrow, and Casca says he will be there. Declaring that "this disturbed sky/ Is not to walk in," Cicero departs.

Comment

Cicero is stoically calm in face of the storm and the fantastic events related by Casca. Casca's credibility is called into question by Cicero's refusal to discuss the meaning of these wonders and in his dispassionate statement that men often err in their interpretations of unnatural phenomena. Casca's report of the Lupercalia may be reexamined in the light of this conversation. Cicero questions Casca's interpretation of events, and so may we.

Casca hears someone coming and issues a challenge. It is Cassius, who recognizes Casca by his voice. Casca asks why the heavens are so menacing. Cassius replies that he has been walking through the storm, exposing himself to the lightning, and asserts that these unnatural events are heaven's instruments of fear and warning that something unnatural is happening on earth. Then he compares the storm to a man no mightier than himself or Casca, a man who roars like a lion in the Capitol. Casca replies, "'Tis Caesar that you mean."

Comment

Having just been advised by Cicero that men tend to interpret events in their own fashion, that is, according to some personal predisposition that they may have, Casca proceeds to ignore this piece of Stoic wisdom and demands an explanation of the wonders from Cassius, the next man he meets in the storm.

Unwittingly confirming Cicero's statement, Cassius explains the monstrous wonders produced during the storm as a warning from heaven that something monstrous is going on earth. The monstrosity he has in mind, of course, is Caesar's ambitious bid for the crown. Cassius may not believe his own interpretation of the supernatural events because he is an epicurean (later in the play he says he has renounced his epicureanism) and does not believe that gods concern themselves with human affairs. He may only be pretending such concern in order to persuade Casca to join the conspiracy. But Cassius, apparently unsuperstitious, has walked "unbraced" (with doublet open), exposing himself to the storm as he intends to face Caesar.

Casca remarks that on the morrow the senators plan to establish Caesar as king over all lands of the empire except Italy. At this Cassius delivers a tirade against tyranny and hurls abuse at the servile Romans for following "so vile a thing as Caesar!" Cassius declares that he is armed and ready to fight Casca should he turn out to be one of Caesar's men. But Casca gives his hand as a pledge of his cooperation, telling Cassius he will join his cause. Cassius then tells Casca that he has already enlisted some of the "noblest-minded Romans" to join him in the deed, "most bloody, fiery and most terrible."

Comment

Although it has been seen that Cassius cannot stomach Caesar's power, that he personally cannot bow to a man who was formerly his equal, we learn from his speech on tyranny that Cassius' feelings are noble ones. It is his methods that are reprehensible, such as the seduction of Brutus from his natural inclinations and the forged letters which he hopes will do the trick.

As Cassius and Casca conclude their pact, Cinna, a member of the conspiracy, arrives. He begins to talk of the storm, but Cassius cuts him short, anxious to know if the conspirators are waiting for him. Cinna says they are and adds how beneficial it would be to their cause if Cassius could "but win the noble Brutus to our party." Cassius orders Cinna to put one of the forged letters on Brutus seat of office, to throw another in his window, and to place a third on the statue of Lucius Junius Brutus (the ancient and heroic namesake of Marcus Brutus). Then Cinna is to meet him at Pompey's theater. Cassius then tells Casca that Brutus is three-parts won to his cause, and at their next encounter he will be entirely persuaded. Casca remarks that Brutus "sits high in all the people's hearts," and that what would appear to be evil if done by them, would appear virtuous if done by Brutus. Cassius agrees with Casca's judgment that Brutus is of great worth and is much needed for their cause, and he bids Casca join him in securing Brutus for their party.

SUMMARY

This scene advances the conspiracy against Caesar. Cassius has already enlisted many noble Romans to his cause, and the plotters are anxious to have Brutus as a "front." In the first scene, we saw the conflict between the people and the Republicans; in the second, the major characters began to take sides in the impending power struggle. In the third, it becomes obvious that the conspiracy against Caesar has grown, and the noblest of the Romans, Brutus, is being drawn into it. The development of Brutus' character continues. In

Scene ii, he was a respected and honorable man, who was hardly aware of his own worth. In this scene, he is judged the most honored of men in Rome who, because of his virtue, can make black appear white. Cassius continues to be characterized as a schemer who is able to manipulate men, but also as one who has a passionate hatred of tyranny and the courage to prefer death to a life of servility.

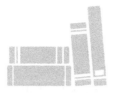

JULIUS CAESAR

ACT II: SCENE I

Review this b/f reading!

Brutus is seen in his orchard at three o'clock in the morning of the ides of March. He cannot sleep because he is troubled by the conflict between his love for Caesar and his love for freedom and Rome. He bids his servant, Lucius, to bring him a candle, and muses over what must be done. He resolves that the only way to stop Caesar is to kill him. Brutus has no personal motive for murdering him; he believes that Caesar must die for the general good. Since he can find nothing in Caesar's past conduct which would justify murder, Brutus projects his thoughts into the future. He considers the possibility of Caesar receiving the crown, changing his nature, and becoming a tyrant. It would be better not to give Caesar this opportunity, not to give the adder its chance to strike. Brutus resolves to "think him as a serpent's egg/ Which, hatch'd, would as his kind grow mischievous,/ And kill him in the shell."

Is this honest? Would someone really kill like this?

Comment

Brutus' soliloquy reveals that he has no personal grievance against Caesar but that he fears Caesar may become a danger to the "general good," the public welfare. He has a strong sense of honor and deep feelings of responsibility to protect the freedom of his native city. Reason as he may, he can find no grounds in Caesar's past behavior for believing that he will abuse his power once he is crowned monarch. Yet, Brutus knows, it is the nature of tyrants to disjoin "remorse from power," that is, to rule without conscience or mercy. So, while he can find nothing in reason to argue against Caesar's coronation, he decides to base his reasoning on possibility. As a monarch, Caesar may run to "extremities" and become excessive in his despotic rule. On the basis of this possibility, which would ruin the Republic, he must be killed. Brutus is an idealist, but he confuses treachery with honor when he decides to kill Caesar for no existing reason.

Lucius reenters with a letter he has found while lighting the candle in Brutus' study. It is the forged note which Cinna has tossed into the window and bears the cryptic message, "Brutus, thou sleepst. Aware, and see thyself!/ Shall Rome, etc. Speak, strike, redress!" Brutus interprets "Shall Rome, etc." to mean "Shall Rome stand under one man's awe?" Lucius returns to report that tomorrow is the fifteenth of March. When the servant leaves to answer a knock at the gate. Brutus continues his thoughts. He says that since Cassius has "whet" him against Caesar, he has not slept a wink. His wakefulness has been a nightmare of conflict between "the genius and the mortal instruments" which work on the human condition as insurrection does on a kingdom.

Comment

The letter contains an ironic comment on Brutus' disturbed condition; it exhorts him to awaken when, in fact, Brutus has not slept since his conversation with Cassius. And like Cassius, he has become dangerous to Caesar, who, we recall, preferred "sleek-headed men, and such as sleep o' nights" (I.ii). Brutus' dangerous line of thinking is made even clearer when he interprets the incomplete but suggestive sentence, "Shall Rome, etc." as a complaint against the potential tyranny of Caesar. The seeds of insurrection, which Cassius had sowed, have taken root in the fertile soil of Brutus' rebellious mind. Brutus' description of the "hideous dream" he is experiencing, in which his mind ("genius") and his body ("mortal instruments") suffer an inner turmoil comparable to the effects of insurrection in a kingdom, reflects the moral philosophy of the Renaissance. In that philosophy the relationship between the body and the mind (or the body and the soul) and the correspondence between the human condition and the body politic were basic assumptions. Shakespeare carefully designed Brutus' personal emotional upheaval to reflect and foreshadow the political chaos which would follow Caesar's assassination.

The word "insurrection" still rings on the stage as Lucius enters to announce the arrival of "your brother Cassius" (Cassius is married to Brutus' sister). Others are with him, but their hats are pulled low over their ears and their faces are buried in cloaks so that they cannot be identified. Brutus comments on the shamefulness of conspiracy that fears to show its monstrous face even in a state full of evil. But he quickly overcomes his sense of shame by reasoning that even if the conspirators continued in their normal ways, the blackness of Erebus (the path to hell) could not hide them from Caesar's tyranny ("prevention").

Cassius, Casca, Decius Brutus, Cinna, Metellus Cimber, and Trebonius enter. Before introducing these men, Cassius tells Brutus that each one is acquainted with and honors him. Brutus and Cassius whisper to each other as the rest of the conspirators engage in small talk, disagreeing over the direction in which the sun is rising. The conclave finished, Brutus takes their hands one by one as fellow conspirators. Cassius proposes that they swear an oath, but Brutus says it is unnecessary, since "the sufferance of our souls, the time's abuse" are strong enough motive to assure their good faith. Honesty and the promise of a Roman is enough, Brutus patriotically asserts.

Comment

Brutus overcomes his natural sense of shame over the idea of conspiracy by using more of the fallacious reasoning which he has already demonstrated in his soliloquy. He allows himself to believe that the evils Caesar may inflict if he becomes monarch actually exist at the moment. However, he shows his own integrity, although misguided, when he rejects Cassius' proposal of the oath. Brutus is convinced that the souls of free men suffer by the "time's abuse" (Caesar's potential coronation), and that the conspirators are all honest Romans nobly concerned with the good of the state.

The apparently insignificant talk about the direction of the rising sun is a humorous and meaningful incident in which Shakespeare characterizes the conspirators as a discordant group who cannot agree on a simple issue and suggests that they are ill-equipped to decide political issues as well.

The oath rejected, Cassius then proposes that Cicero be included in their group. Casca and Cinna agree, and Metellus

Cimber reasons that Cicero's dignity and age will win them the good opinion of the masses. "It shall be said his judgment rul'd our hands," Cimber states. Brutus rejects Cassius' second proposal, arguing that Cicero "will never follow anything/ That other men begin." Cassius grudgingly agrees to leave Cicero out. Decius proposes to kill Antony as well as Caesar. Cassius readily agrees, on the grounds that Antony is a "shrewd contriver" and may well harm them later. For a third time, Brutus opposes Cassius on the grounds that "Antony is but a limb of Caesar. / Let us be sacrificers, but not butchers. As for Caesar, "Let's carve him as a dish fit for the gods,/ Not hew him as a carcass fit for hounds." Naively, Brutus adds, "We shall be call'd purgers, not murderers. And for Mark Antony, think not of him;/ For he can do no more than Caesar's arm/ When Caesar's head is off."

Comment

Brutus has taken Antony's love of pleasure and his loyalty to Caesar as a sign of political weakness. He conceives of the murder of Caesar as a religious sacrifice rather than a slaughter and is blind to the possibility that his sacrifice may, in fact, be sacrilege, because the gods have ordained that Caesar rule. Brutus also fails to realize that, although he personally may be fearful of Caesar's power, the people are not. He is acting out of a patrician and Stoic sense of duty to the state, which according to his philosophy is the highest motive from which men may act.

Unlike Brutus, Cassius observes and understands men. He perceives that Antony is a "shrewd contriver" and that he has a large force which, if increased, could endanger the conspirators' cause. Cassius errs against his own judgments by acceding to each of Brutus' three decisions. *Why would Cassius do this?*

The clock strikes three, and Trebonius says it is time to part. Cassius finds it doubtful that Caesar will come forth because of the "apparent prodigies" and unaccustomed terrors of the night, "for he is superstitious grown of late." But Decius promises to get Caesar to the Capitol by flattering him with praise of his hatred for flatterers. Cassius proposes that instead, all the conspirators go and fetch Caesar. Metellus Cimber bids them include Caius Ligarius in the plot, and Brutus assents, asking that, Caius Ligarius be sent to him. Their plans concluded, the conspirators adjourn. Brutus calls his servant, but finding him asleep, he tenderly wishes him sweet dreams and reflects on the sound slumber of those unburdened by care.

Comment

In Elizabethan philosophy, superstition was a sign of the diseased senses. Thus, by calling Caesar superstitious, Cassius adds to the portrait of Caesar as a decaying and declining man. Caesar's susceptibility to flattery suggests that his moral sense is decaying as well as his mental power.

Brutus' address to Lucius his servant expresses his affection for the boy and reveals his own gentle nature. Shakespeare frequently uses the unburdened sleep of humble people as a contrast to the restless state of the leaders of men, particularly insurgents.

When the conspirators have gone, Brutus' wife, Portia, comes to inquire why Brutus is up in the middle of the night. She wants to know what has been absorbing him so much of late. Brutus replies that he is not well. Portia retorts that Brutus is not acting like someone sick in body but like someone with a troubled spirit. She implores him on her knees to tell her what is wrong and asks about the visitors who had come in with their faces hidden. She declares that by failing to share his secret, Brutus excludes her from part of the marriage and makes her his harlot rather than his wife. Brutus insists she is his honorable wife, but Portia continues to protest her good repute, by virtue of her father, the noble Cato, and by her own act of courage, a self-inflicted thigh would that was intended to prove her worth as Brutus' wife and the sharer of his secrets.

Comment

The **theme** of disease is continued in this dialogue in Brutus' feigned excuse for his behavior and in Portia's accurate and ironical diagnosis that there is "some sick offense within your mind." Physical and mental diseases repeatedly figure as symbols of the disease of civil rebellion, which Caesar's murder and its results represent.

The nobility and courage of Portia are expressed in this passage. She is the daughter of Marcus Porcius Cato, who killed himself at the battle of Utica in the civil war against Caesar rather than fall into Caesar's hands. Plutarch wrote that Portia cut her thigh with a razor to prove her courage, and this is undoubtedly the meaning of her "voluntary wound" in the thigh.

Brutus is touched by his wife's devotion and is about to tell her his plans when he is interrupted by the entrance of Ligarius. Ligarius has been ill but is ready to throw his bandages aside if Brutus proposes some exploit worthy of the name of honor. Brutus says such an exploit is planned, and at these words, Ligarius throws aside his bandages and presents himself ready for action. Brutus says that the plot is one which will make sick men whole and that he will tell Ligarius of it as they walk.

Ligarius replies that even though he is ignorant of the plot, it is enough for him that Brutus leads it.

Comment

The **theme** of sickness or disease is continued in this interview. Ligarius, literally ill, says he will become well when a deed of honor is proposed. Caesar's later remark that Ligarius' illness has made him lean (like dangerous men) is a dramatically ironic reference to Ligarius' statement here. Equally ironic is the fact that the plot against Caesar which should make "sick men whole" has disturbed Brutus' quiet mind and turned it from health to sickness. The entire conspiracy is, thus, associated with the disease of insurrection, and Caesar's own rule is given a similar unhealthy cast through its association with the infirmities of Caesar.

SUMMARY

The main purpose of this scene is to show the change which takes place in Brutus after his first conversation with Cassius. The seeds of insurrection having been planted. Brutus is torn by inner conflict as he decides to join and head the conspiracy. His motives are honorable, but he mistakes treachery for honesty and murder for sacrifice. He finds oaths unnecessary among noble Roman; he vetoes an invitation to Cicero to join the conspiracy, and he objects to Antony's murder, underestimating the shrewdness and potential danger in the man. Each of these judgments is based on high civic and moral principles, and, in contrast with Cassius' suggestions, they are impractical and unrealistic, as we shall see.

The conspirators show their true colors when they disagree over a trifling matter such as the direction of the sun's rising and when they invite Ligarius to join the conspiracy because he hates Caesar, not because he loves Rome. Their desire to enlist Cicero for the dignity he will bring their "youths and wildness" is similar to the reason for choosing Brutus for the virtue with which he will coat their offenses (I. iii).

Cassius shows skill in judging men and opposes the naive decisions of Brutus. Nevertheless, he is influenced by Brutus' principled behavior and betrays his own judgment in yielding to Brutus' wishes. The noble and courageous Portia is introduced in this scene, and her reference to Cato her father (who fought for Pompey against Caesar) suggests that she will endorse her husband's plot.

ACT II: SCENE II

The storm is still raging as the scene shifts to Caesar's house. It is three A. M. in the morning of the ides of March. Caesar, like Brutus, is spending a restless night. He exclaims that neither heaven nor earth is peaceful on this night; even Calpurnia, his wife, is having disturbed dreams and has cried out three times in her sleep, "Help, ho! They murder Caesar!" Caesar sends a servant to the priests and orders them to make a sacrifice and send him the results. Calpurnia enters and begs Caesar not to stir out of the house that day, but Caesar fatalistically replies, "What can be avoided Whose end is purposed by the mighty gods?"

Calpurnia says that she is not normally upset by prodigies, but that the unnatural occurrences of the proceeding night have disturbed her: a lioness was seen giving birth in the streets; the dead rose from their graves; and fiery warriors fought in the clouds so fiercely that blood drizzled upon the Capitol. There were also reports that horses neighed. that dying men groaned, and that ghosts shrieked and squealed along the streets.

Comment

The appearance of the lioness, the warriors, and the dying men are **foreshadowings** of Caesar's death and the civil chaos which will follow his death. Caesar's resigned acceptance of the will of the gods is the position taken by the Stoic philosophers who purged their minds of all fear and passion to leave them free for virtuous thought and action.

Calpurnia interprets the comets in the air, also seen during the night, as a prophecy of the death of a prince, for comets are never seen when beggars die. Caesar firmly encourages his wife with the now famous lines, "Cowards die many times before their deaths;/ The valiant never taste of death but once." He finds it strange that men should have fears, since death is a necessity which "will come when it will come."

Comment

Calpurnia's superstitious interpretations of the wonders of the night express her fears for Caesar's life; they are projections of the thoughts which trouble her most just as Cassius' interpretation of the prodigies reflect his greatest fear, that Caesar will become king. Caesar's courage is asserted here; it is the characteristic courage of a man who has known war and conquest and is confident of his own bravery. But Caesar also shows that he has lost touch with ordinary men and no longer understands their passions.

Calpurnia's dream has already foreshadowed Caesar's murder, and the dramatic **irony** of the situation continues as she warns Caesar not to leave the house and Caesar replies that the only real threats that can be made to him are those made to his back, that is, through conspiracy, which is now being organized behind his back.

The sacrifice Caesar had ordered earlier has been done, and the servant returns to report that the priests advise Caesar to stay at home, for the beast, when opened, was found to have no heart. Caesar defies this answer of the gods sent by the priests, and like Cassius and Calpurnia, he gives his own interpretation of the sacrifice, which is colored by his personal predilections. The heartless beast, Caesar asserts, is a chastisement of the gods against cowardice. If he should stay at home this day, Caesar would be a beast without a heart. (The heart was regarded as the seat of courage in Renaissance physiology and philosophy.) He calls himself the brother of danger; metaphorically, he and danger are two lions born on the same day, and of the two, Caesar is the more terrible. (The lion, the king of the beasts, traditionally represented the king of men, the masculine spirit, and male courage.) "Caesar shall go forth," the intemperate ruler declares.

Comment

Caesar's defiance of the priests and of the gods themselves is immoderate and even blasphemous. His judgment fails when he sacrilegiously defies the advice of the priests and the "ceremonies" (religious superstitions) which frighten Calpurnia. He is, indeed, tempting the gods, and his fate awaits him.

The likeness of men and animals was the basis of the study of physiognomy during the Renaissance, and the lion **metaphor** repeatedly reflects this habit of comparison. Cassius, Calpurnia, and now Caesar himself interpret the appearance of the lion in the Capitol as the animal corresponding symbolically to Caesar.

When Caesar declares himself braver than danger itself, Calpurnia exclaims that Caesar is losing sight of his wisdom in his overconfidence. She implores him to send Mark Antony to the Senate to say Caesar is not well. According to her "humor," Caesar agrees to send the message and to remain at home.

Comment

The reason for Caesar's concession to Calpurnia's fears has been a point of critical contention. Either Caesar is hiding his real fears by seeming to consent to Calpurnia's "humor" or he means just what he says and grants his wife's wish out of tenderness for her. (Brutus in a parallel scene with his wife also grants her wish, although his granting of it does not become apparent immediately.) Calpurnia's accusation that Caesar has become overconfident is the first clear indication that Caesar has been afflicted with that state of mad arrogance which in ancient Greek theology was believed to arouse the wrath of Nemesis, the goddess of moderation who hated every transgression of the bounds of temperance and restored the proper and normal order of all things through chastisement and vengeance.

Decius Brutus enters to fetch Caesar to the Senate. Caesar asks Decius to bear his greeting to the senators and tell them that he will not come today. He adds that to say he cannot come is false, and to say he dares not come is even falser. Calpurnia tells Decius to say that Caesar is sick, but Caesar insists that he will not send a lie. He bids Decius again to say simply that he will not come. Craftily, Decius asks Caesar to give him some cause so that Decius will not be laughed at when he delivers the message. Arrogantly, Caesar answers that it is enough to tell the Senate that Caesar will not come, but because he loves Decius, for his personal satisfaction, he will give him the reason: Calpurnia keeps him at home because she dreamed she saw his statue like a fountain with a hundred spouts, pouring forth blood in which smiling Romans bathed their hands.

Decius protests that Calpurnia's dream has been misinterpreted, that it really means that Rome sucks reviving blood from Caesar and through him regains its vitality. Decius adds that the Senate has decided to give Caesar a crown this day. If he does not come, the Senate may change its mind. Decius argues that the dream as a reason for his absence "were a mock/ Apt to be rendered for someone to say/ 'Break up the Senate till another time,/ When Caesar's wife shall meet with better dreams." That is, Caesar's excuse might be interpreted as an insult by one of the senators. Furthermore, if Caesar does not appear, senators will say that Caesar is afraid. Caesar is persuaded to see that Calpurnia's fears are foolish ones and tells his wife to get his robes, for he will go.

Comment

Caesar is a man of personal tenderness as well as public ambition, courage, and virtue. Personally unafraid, he is nevertheless capable of conceding to the fears and wishes of those he loves. Such softness at this point in his life is a sign of his age and growing infirmity, for the conquering hero of Caesar's youth was more decisive and more firm in his convictions. It has been argued that Caesar's words are not to be trusted and that he is really a frightened man, covering his fears with a show of bravado, and using Calpurnia as an excuse to act out his own cowardly inclinations. Decius' argument may then be interpreted as the crafty manipulation of an arrogant, conceited, and fearful old man.

Publius, Brutus, Ligarius, Metellus, Casca, Trebonius, and Cinna enter to escort Caesar to the Senate, and Caesar graciously welcomes them. Alluding to their former enmity, Caesar also notes that Ligarius' illness has made him lean. The clock strikes eight as Antony enters. Caesar remarks that despite the fact that Antony revels all night, he is able to get up in time for his duties in the morning. Caesar apologizes for keeping his escorts waiting and bids Cinna, Metellus, and Trebonius to sit near him in the Senate. Trebonius replies in an aside that he will be so near Caesar that Caesar's best friends will wish he had been further away. Caesar invites the men to drink wine with him and then "like friends," they shall be off together. In response to Caesar's show of trust, Brutus mourns, in an aside, that every "like" is not the "same."

Comment

Caesar is portrayed among his apparent friends as a gracious, polished and courteous host. (He is neither arrogant nor pompous as in his other appearances.) When Brutus sees Caesar behave in his usual generous and gracious manner, his personal love for Caesar comes to the fore, and he grieves ("earns") over Caesar's assumption that they are all "like friends" Punning on several meanings of the word "like" (love, the same as, apparent), Brutus regrets that all meanings of "like" are not "same," and that all loving friends are not what they appear to be, nor do they remain the "same" in their loyalty. Caesar's wish that the conspirators remains close to him in the Senate is another instance of dramatic **irony**, for as Trebonius implies in his aside (intended only for the audience's hearing), he will be close enough to murder Caesar.

SUMMARY

This crucial scene serves many purposes in advancing the plot and characterizations of the major figures. First, this scene is carefully balanced with the one immediately preceding in which Brutus meets with the conspirators and with his wife Portia. Here Caesar and his devoted wife Calpurnia are seen, then the conspirators arrive as guests. Like Portia, Calpurnia petitions her husband on her knees and at first wins her point that he remain at home. Like Portia, Calpurnia is fearful, restless, concerned for her husband. Both wives are well-suited to their husbands. Portia and Brutus are young, strong, and courageous; Calpurnia and Caesar are aging, infirm, and superstitious.

Both Brutus and Caesar entertain the same guests. Ironically, however, the guests arrive in friendship in Brutus' garden, concealed by hats and cloaks, to form a conspiratorial alliance, while the same men visit Caesar as enemies, wearing no disguise at all. They simply mask their monstrous visages under "smiles and affability" as Brutus had planned in the preceding scene (II. i. 85-6).

Both Brutus and Caesar are seen as tender and yielding husbands and gracious and courteous hosts. Both trust the honesty of the conspirators; both succumb to their flattery. Brutus, however misguided, relies on his reason and his sense of duty, and is firmly decisive in dealing with the plans for the assassination. Caesar's behavior has been vacillating in dealing with the omen of Calpurnia's dream and the advice of the priests whose augurs he had demanded. The assured rashness of Brutus' youth in the preceding scene is contrasted with the vacillation and overconfidence of the aging Caesar in the present scene.

The **themes** of prodigies, dreams, augurs, and their interpretations are carried on in this scene, establishing an atmosphere of unrest, insurrection, and foreboding which is so essential to the building of suspense for the crucial murder scene and the subsequent events.

ACT II: SCENE III

64/17 Start the review here!

In a street near the Capitol, Artemidorus appears reading a paper. Artemidorus places himself in a spot where Caesar must pass on his walk to the Capitol, and rereads the letter he plans to thrust into Caesar's hands. The letter warns Caesar to beware of Brutus, Cassius, Casca, Cinna, and other members of the conspiracy because they are plotting against his life. It warns Caesar that unless he is immortal, overconfidence opens the way for conspiracy. His letter ends, "If thou read this, O Caesar; thou mayst live;/ If not, the Fates with traitors do contrive."

Comment And Summary

Artemidorus was a "doctor of rhetoric in the Greek language, who, because of his profession, associated with certain of Brutus' confederates, knew most of their practices against Caesar," according to Plutarch. This explains how Artemidorus was in a position to learn of the plot. Suspense is created by establishing the fact that the plot against Caesar is in danger of failure. The letter suggests that Caesar's failure to recognize the conspiracy will be a result of hubris or overconfidence, of presuming to be immortal like the gods, who alone are secure in their immortality. Calpurnia has already warned Caesar against overconfidence, but he has chosen to ignore her. This presumptuous sense of security on Caesar's part will prevent him from reading the second warning.

ACT II: SCENE IV

On the morning of the ides of March, Portia stands before the house of Brutus, directing her servant Lucius to run to the Senate House. Having been informed of the assassination plot by Brutus, she is visibly distraught over the possible danger to her husband should his plans miscarry. The boy asks what errand he is to perform at the Senate, and Portia realizes that she cannot tell. How hard it is for a woman to keep a secret, Portia reflects, for although she has a man's mind, she has only a woman's might. The bewildered servant asks if he must run to the Capitol and back again and do nothing else, but Portia, now composed, orders him to bring her word if Brutus looks well, for he seemed sick when he left.

[handwritten margin note: where is this in the text?]

Portia imagines she hears a "bustling rumor" (uproar, report) from the Capitol, but it is only the Soothsayer who arrives on his way to the Capitol. Hoping to get news of him, Portia asks the Soothsayer which way he has been, but when she learns that he has just come from home, she asks him the time and inquires whether or not Caesar has gone to the Capitol. The Soothsayer replies that Caesar has not gone yet; he adds that he himself is going to find a place to see Caesar pass on the way to the Senate. Portia wants to know if he has a suit with Caesar, to which, he replies that he is going to "beseech him to befriend himself." Fearfully, Portia asks if the Soothsayer knows of any harm intended toward Caesar, and she is told that the

Soothsayer knows of no harm intended but fears there will be some. He excuses himself, saying that he must find a good spot before the crowds gather.

After he leaves, Portia complains about the weakness of the woman's heart, "O Brutus!/ The heavens speed thee in thine enterprise." Fearing that the boy has overheard her prayer, she adds that "Brutus hath a suit/ That Caesar will not grant." She grows faint and, forgetting her former errand, tells the boy to run to Brutus, inform him that she is well, and return with word of what he says.

Comment And Summary

This brief scene serves as another stage in the building of suspense for the crucial action of the assassination. The dramatization of Portia's anxiety creates a sympathetic emotional response to her own impatience and fears over the outcome of the plot, as she nearly gives the plans away several times during this brief interval. The arrival of the Soothsayer and the disclosure of his prophetic warning adds to the cumulative effect of the suspense which is being created. The prophet's warning to Caesar in the following scene is prepared for at this point, and it is seen that Caesar will have still another opportunity to "befriend himself," as mortals must. By the time that Caesar overconfidently rejects each of the warnings prepared for him, it will be clearly understood that Caesar has been chastised (warned by the gods) and that vengeance is in order. Caesar, as much as Brutus, is responsible for his own tragic fate.

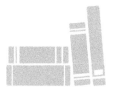

JULIUS CAESAR

. . . .

ACT III: SCENE I

The Conspirators escort Caesar to the capital.

Brutus, Cassius, Casca, Decius Brutus, Metellus, Trebonius, Cinna, Antony, Lepidus, Popilius, Peblius, and others accompany Caesar through the streets to the Capitol. A crowd has gathered to watch the procession, among them Artemidorus and the Soothsayer. As Caesar and his train pass, Caesar sees the Soothsayer in the crowd and confidently reminds him that "the Ides of March are come." "Ay, Caesar," replies the Soothsayer, "but not gone." Artemidorus then comes forward and begs Caesar to read his note, but Decius hastily intervenes with another note, asking Caesar to read Trebonius' suit at his leisure. Impetuously, Artemidorus demands that Caesar read his first, for it is of personal importance to Caesar. Magnanimously, Caesar replies, what concerns Caesar himself will be read last. When Artemidorus insists again, Caesar indignantly exclaims, "What! is this fellow mad?" Cassius steps in and chides Artemidorus for presenting petitions in the streets; the Capitol is the proper place for such requests.

Comment

Caesar has just gone down for the third time. He has overruled Calpurnia's fears, confidently mocked the Soothsayer, and now indignantly rejects Artemidorus' plea that Caesar think of himself. His arrogance on these matters is his own contribution to the tragedy which must now ensue.

Caesar goes up to the Senate House, followed by the crowd. Popilius whispers good luck to Cassius on his enterprise, but when the startled Cassius asks, "What enterprise, Popilius?" the senator simply replies, "Fare you well" and advances toward Caesar. Cassius tells Brutus of Popilius' ambiguous remarks and expresses his fear that their conspiracy has been discovered. He vows that if the plot is unsuccessful, he will kill himself. Brutus tells Cassius to be calm, for Popilius is smiling as he talks to Caesar and Caesar's face shows no sign of change.

Comment

Popilius' ambiguous remark brings the play to its height of suspense, for Cassius' guilty conscience causes him to give the most fearful interpretation to the senator's good wishes. As Popilius walks to Caesar's side and speaks to him, attention is focused on Cassius who watches Caesar. The fear of disclosure makes Cassius vow his own death, but at the peak of excitement, Brutus reads Caesar and the senator's faces. Be calm, Brutus urges, and we learn that the plot is still on. (According to Plutarch, Popilius told Cassius that their enterprise had already been betrayed, but Shakespeare, who certainly knew this historical report, artfully rephrases Popilius' words so that their ambiguity will create a most intense dramatic moment.)

Cassius notices that the plan is beginning to work, for Trebonius is drawing Antony out of the way. Antony and Trebonius leave as the senators take their seats. Cassius asks for Metellus Cimber so that he can present his suit to Caesar, while Brutus urges the conspirators to press near Caesar and aid Metellus. Cinna tells Casca that he is to be the first one to strike Caesar. As Caesar calls the Senate to order, Metellus kneels before Caesar and begins a flattering address. Caesar cuts him short with a lengthy reply in which he asserts that Caesar is not like ordinary men who succumb to flattery and make childish decisions. He cannot be melted by praise from the "true quality" of a suit. He says that if Metellus is pleading for his brother who has been banished, Caesar will "spurn thee like a cur out of my way." Metellus asks if anyone else will aid his suit for his banished brother. Brutus comes forward and kisses Caesar's hand, saying that he does this not in flattery, but out of desire for Caesar to repeal the banishment of Publius Cimber. Next, Cassius humbly entreats Caesar, falling "low as to thy foot." But Caesar remains adamant.

In a piece of over-extended self-eulogy Caesar asserts, "I am constant as the Northern Star,/ Of whose true-fixed and resting quality/ There is no fellow in the firmament." Among men on earth, Caesar continues, "men are flesh and blood, and apprehensive;/ Yet in the number I do know but one/ That unassailable holds on his rank,/ Unshaked of motion; and that I am he." Publius Cimber shall remain banished, for Caesar cannot be moved. Cinna and Decius implore Caesar, but he dismisses them, uttering the most arrogant statement of all, "Hence! Wilt thou lift up Olympus?" Casca signals the attack, "Speak, hands,

[handwritten margin note: Cassca is the 1st to Strike at—Unreasoning! Casca is urging!]

for me!" He stabs Caesar, and one by one, the other conspirators add their blows. Seeing Brutus among their number, the stricken Caesar cries, "*Et tu, Brute?* Then fall, Caesar."

Comment

The assassination is one of the most dramatic moments on the Shakespearean stage. Metellus begins the action by petitioning for his brother's repeal from banishment. One by one, the conspirators join in the plea, kneeling abject and humble before the merciless ruler who shuns their petitions with arrogant boasts of his own firmness of decision and constancy. As Caesar extravagantly compares himself to the northern star, he is surrounded by kneeling figures who seem to inflate the already immoderate sense of his own worth. Caesar's self-praise grows stronger and more intemperate; he above all men is "unassailable." The assailants bide their time. Ignobly dismissed by Caesar, who now reaches the height of arrogance and blasphemy as he likens himself to an Olympian god, Casca signals the attack.

Caesar's merciless response to his petitioners, his abuse of power, his arrogant self-praise, have worked on the passions of the audience as well as the conspirators, and Casca's death blow comes as a welcome relief from the madness of self-inflation which Caesar has imparted. Once stricken, however, Caesar becomes the object of total sympathy. "*Et tu, Brute?*" Even you, Brutus, The pathetic query of the fallen leader, three words, counteracts all the injury Caesar has done by his outrageously hubristic boasts. His friend's betrayal ends his will to live. "Then fall, Caesar." From this point on, Caesar's sins will be forgotten and only his noblest attributes will be remembered, suggesting that the play may be pointing to a political lesson, that a tyrant, however intolerable, is a force against disorder, which is far worse than tyranny.

As Caesar dies, the senators and people retreat in confusion. Cinna cries out, "Liberty! Freedom! Tyranny is dead!/ Run hence, proclaim, cry it about the streets." Cassius bids the conspirators to run to the common pulpits and call out "Liberty, freedom, and enfranchisement!" Casca encourages Brutus to go to the pulpit, and Decius urges Cassius to go also. Brutus and Cassius advise the senator Publius to leave, lest the people attack the conspirators and harm the aged senator. Brutus adds that no man should bear the consequences of the deed, except the conspirators themselves. Trebonius returns and tells his fellows that Antony had fled to his house amazed and that "Men, wives, and children stare, cry out, and run,/ As it were doomsday."

Brutus asks the Fates what is in store for the assassins now. Agreeing with Cassius that life involves the fear of death, Brutus declares that they are Caesar's friends for having cut off his life from years of fearing death. Then Brutus exhorts the conspirators to bathe their hands and arms in Caesar's blood, and with their swords besmeared with the blood, to walk into the market place, shouting "Peace, freedom, liberty!" Cassius envisions that in ages to come this noble scene will be enacted by nations yet unborn and in languages yet unknown. Brutus wonders how many times plays will be held portraying the bleeding of Caesar, who now lies by Pompey's statue, "No worthier than the dust!" And Cassius adds that in these plays of the future, they will be remembered as the men who gave liberty to their country.

Comment

The chaos and disorder which reigns immediately after the assassination is narrated by the conspirators. The silently amazed Publius, venerable senator of the Republic, represents the astounded confusion of the general public. Brutus' noble concern for Publius' age and safety, even in the passionate aftermath of the slaughter, reveals the truly noble nature of the man, as does his claiming responsibility for the assassination and his willingness to yield to the decision of the Fates. Brutus' exhortation to the blood-bath is not expressive of the blood lust of the man but of his desire to treat the assassination as a sacrifice by the ritualistic smearing of the victim's blood on the priests of liberty and by showing the public that an offering has been made in the name of "Peace, freedom, and liberty."

Infused by the lofty purpose of their deed, Cassius and Brutus envision themselves as heroes of liberty who will be immortalized on the stages of nations (like England), which are yet unformed. Thus, the effects of the murder are shown from two points of view. The senate and the public flee in confusion or are paralyzed by astonishment, while the conspirators are inspired by the lofty purpose of their deed, which they imagine has ennobled their names and will receive the acclaim of all posterity.

The structural unity imparted to the play by the device of the dream and the arrangement of events is embedded in this scene. The blood-bath fulfills and explains Calpurnia's dream of the statue pouring blood, and the death of Caesar at the foot of Pompey's statue complements the initial reference in the play to Caesar's triumph over Pompey's blood. Visually, the statue of Pompey can now be seen standing in triumph over Caesar's blood.

Just as the conspirators have decided to leave the Senate House with Brutus at their head, a servant of Antony's arrives. The servant says that Antony instructed him to kneel before Brutus and deliver the message that Antony loves and honors Brutus, that he feared, honored, and loved Caesar, and if Brutus can show him why Caesar deserved to die, "Mark Antony shall not love Caesar dead/ So well as Brutus living; but will follow/ The fortunes and affairs of noble Brutus." Brutus at once replies that his master is a wise and valiant Roman. He instructs the slave to fetch Antony to the Capitol to learn the cause of Caesar's murder and to tell him that by Brutus' honor, he will depart unharmed. While the servant runs to get Antony, Cassius tells Brutus that he fears Antony and that his fears very often prove correct.

Antony arrives, and ignoring Brutus, he addresses Caesar's body, "O mighty Caesar! Dost thou lie so low?/ Are all thy conquests, glories, triumphs, spoils,/ Shrunk to this little measure?" Then Antony asks who else must die and says that if he is marked for death, he will never be more ready than now. If he lived a thousand years, he would find no place, no hour, no weapon more pleasing than those which have accompanied Caesar's death, nor would he find executioners more fitting than those who are now "the choice and master spirits of this age."

Comment

Antony's arrival on the scene of the crime is partly out of loyalty to his master Caesar and partly out of the desire to effect a reconciliation with the assassins until he can muster the force to oppose them successfully. Although he says he is prepared to die, he has first made certain through his servant that Brutus promises him safe conduct. His flattering address to the killers then may be interpreted as the first cautious step in a counter-rebellion, and Cassius' misgivings over Antony seem to be falling "shrewdly to the purpose," to be proving true. Antony from this point on begins to display the dangerous and shrewd political judgment which Cassius has perceived in him. He is more than the lover of plays and music and all-night revels; he will be seen to be as calculating as Cassius, as persuasive as Decius Brutus, as noble and far more loyal than Brutus.

Brutus tells Antony not to beg for death, for although the conspirators appear to be bloody and cruel, their hearts are actually filled with pity for the general wrong done to Rome by Caesar. Antony is welcome to join their ranks. Cassius adds that Antony will have as much power to dispense favors in the new state as the conspirators do. Brutus asks Antony to await an explanation patiently until the people, who are beside themselves with fear, have been appeased; then he will explain why he who loved Caesar struck him down.

Comment

* Brutus is idealistic

Once again we see the sharp contrast between Brutus and Cassius. The idealistic Brutus has been explaining Caesar's murder and Antony's welcome in terms of "our hearts" and "all kind love, good thoughts, and reverence." On the other hand, the practical Cassius realizes these words mean little to Antony and offers him some of the powers the insurgents have won.

Pretending to be satisfied with the assassins' wisdom in overthrowing Caesar, Antony takes the bloody hand of each of the men. Antony realizes that to the conspirators he must appear to be either a coward or a flatterer, and turning to the dead body of Caesar, he begs its forgiveness for befriending Caesar's enemies. He declares how unbecoming it is to the love he bore Caesar to make peace with the assassins in the very sight of the corpse; it would be more fitting to weep at the fall of Caesar, whom Antony now compares to a noble deer, run down and killed by a pack of hounds.

Cassius interrupts Antony's apology to Caesar, at which Antony begs his pardon for praising the dead man before his slayers. Still, Antony points out, his praise is slight; Caesar's enemies will do him as much credit. In a friend, however, Antony's words are merely passionless understatement. But Cassius is not prepared to blame Antony for praising Caesar; what he wants to know is can Antony be counted on as one of his allies, or shall the conspirators go along their way without depending on Antony's support. Antony explains that he shook their hands in order to indicate his alliance with their cause, but the sight of Caesar did indeed sway him from that resolution. Therefore, Antony qualifies his pledge of friendship; he will join their ranks if they are able to supply reasons why and in what way Caesar was dangerous. Brutus promises that the reasons he will give Antony would satisfy him even if he were the son of Caesar himself.

Comment

Antony's eulogy over the body of Caesar includes a simile in which Caesar is compared to a hart and his murderers to hounds. The figure, however covert to the conspirators, is that Antony has likened them to dogs. We shall see shortly that this is exactly how he feels about them.

There may be a touch of historical irony in Brutus' promise to give reasons so satisfactory that even a son of Caesar would be satisfied. Although in this play Shakespeare makes no use of the

[handwritten margin note: Anthony asks the conspirators of proof of Caesar's threat!?]

fact that Caesar and Brutus' mother were lovers during the time when Brutus was born, the phrasing of Brutus' promise may be a subtle allusion to the unconfirmed report that Brutus was Caesar's bastard son.

Antony asks if he can deliver the funeral oration over Caesar's body in the market-place. Without any hesitation, Brutus agrees to Antony's request. Cassius pulls Brutus aside and cautions him not to allow Antony to speak. "You know not what you do," Cassius warns. Antony easily may stir up the people. Convinced of the justice of his crime, Brutus answers that he will speak first and tell the people the reasons for the murder of Caesar, and that Antony speaks with their permission, since they want Caesar to have "true rites and lawful ceremonies." Brums is sure "it shall advantage more than do us wrong." Cassius says he still doesn't like it. Brutus then orders Antony not to blame the conspirators during his oration, but to speak good of Caesar without condemning his killers. Furthermore, he is to say he speaks with the insurgents' permission, and he must agree to speak after Brutus. Antony assents, and Brutus bids him to prepare the body and follow them. The conspirators go off, leaving Antony alone with the body.

Comment

Brutus is not a subtle man; he cannot imagine that Antony may be lying about joining their cause. Besides, he has such confidence in his own powers of reasoning that he believes he can convince Antony, the people, and even Caesar's son, if he had one, of the justice of his deed. Cassius continues to be suspicious and finds it more and more difficult to concur with Brutus' decisions. His strongest arguments, however, are based on feelings not reasons, and his only course in view of Brutus' idealism is to submit to it entirely.

Alone with the body, Antony speaks his true feelings to the corpse. He begs pardon for being so meek and gentle with Caesar's butchers. "Thou art the ruins of the noblest man/ That ever lived in the tide of time," Antony declares. He swears an oath so strong that he calls it "prophecy" over the gaping wounds of Caesar which "like dumb mouths, do open their ruby lips/ To beg the voice and utterance of my tongue." The limbs of men shall be cursed for Caesar's death, domestic fury and civil strife shall spread through Italy. Blood, destruction, and other monstrosities of war will become such a familiar sight in the land that mothers will merely smile when they see their infants cut up by the hands of war, Caesar's spirit, with Ate (the hellish god of discord) at his side, shall range through the land and "Cry 'Havoc.'" And "this foul deed shall smell above the earth/ With carrion men, groaning for burial."

Comment

The soliloquy reveals Antony's true purpose in seeming to befriend the conspirators. He is eager to give his prince a ceremonial burial before he musters forces and ranges through the land carrying destruction to the farthest reaches until Caesar's death has been avenged. The imagery in this speech is, perhaps, the most revolting imagery to be found in Shakespeare. It is designed to show the full extent of Antony's hatred and rage against "this foul deed." The images of civil chaos are grotesque and grisly in the extreme; mother's smiling at their quartered babes and dead men rotting above the ground, crying out for burials, are the horrible conceptions of an impassioned brain.

These are the feelings of Antony as he looks at the gaping wounds of Caesar, which seem to him like repulsive yet appealing ruby lips, begging Antony for revenge.

Once more Cassius' suspicions fall "shrewdly to the purpose"; Antony intends to betray his new-made friendship. Brutus' judgment has been wrong again. There can be no good reasons to satisfy the angry spirit Antony has just displayed. The remainder of the play is foreshadowed by Antony's "prophecy"; civil strife and destruction will follow; Caesar's spirit will seek revenge.

Antony's harangue is ended by the arrival of a messenger whom Antony recognizes as the servant of Octavius Caesar. The messenger begins to relay his message, but when he sees the body of Caesar, he cries out. Tears welling in his eyes, Antony asks the slave if his master is coming and learns that Octavius is only seven leagues from Rome. Antony orders the slave to tell his master what has happened and to warn him that Rome is not safe for entry. On second thought, Antony decides to have the servant wait until after the funeral oration. After they see how the people react to the murder, the slave may report to Octavius on the state of things. Then Antony and the servant carry Caesar's body off.

Comment

A new character, Octavius Caesar, is introduced just at the point when Julius Caesar is carried off. Octavius was the grand-nephew of Caesar, his son by adoption, and his first heir. He actually arrived in Rome a month after Caesar's demise and took his name Caesar only after he heard the terms of his uncle's will. His arrival at this point, however, as another Caesar, has obvious dramatic significance; he is meant to convey the idea that "Caesar" is not dead. (The king is dead; long live the king.) Octavius is generally known as Augustus (the revered one) after the title given him later by the people of Rome. Shakespeare ignores the exact chronology of historical facts, although he knew them well, because adherence to them would clearly interfere with the development of the plot and destroy the dramatic effect and thematic significance of Octavius' timely arrival.

SUMMARY

This scene brings the play to its first climax. The first two acts dealt with the events leading up to Caesar's death; the remainder of the play deals with the events leading to the death of Cassius and Brutus. The stage is set here for the action which follows the assassination.

Once Caesar has been killed, the focus of the play shifts to Brutus, whereas it has previously been on Caesar as well as Brutus. Brutus has been shown as a noble, honorable, and virtuous man who, because of these very qualities, is blind to reality and practicality. Brutus' role now changes from conspirator to victim, hunter to fugitive, and Antony's role expands as he plans action against Brutus. Brutus' blindness becomes more and more evident after this point. Caesar's excessive courage had made him blind to the normal precautions taken by men, while Brutus' excessive idealism now obscures his view of the practical reality of politics. Brutus' stubborn naiveté, his tragic flaw, leads to his destruction, for his quick acceptance of Antony's friendship, despite the warnings of Cassius, is neither the first nor the last mistake in judgment that Brutus makes.

In this scene, Antony emerges as a loyal friend, but he is also a wily, conniving, vengeful, and ambitious man. He declares that he will plunge all Italy into civil war in order to avenge Caesar and actually does this in the play, while Brutus has been anxious that only the conspirators suffer for the assassination.

The death of Caesar so early in the play raises a legitimate question: Who is the main character of *Julius Caesar?* Some critics maintain that Caesar is the focus of the entire play, the man being replaced by the spirit or ghost of Caesar after the assassination. Others insist that Brutus is the real tragic hero, that the focus is on him throughout the play, that the assassination is the first climax of his career, and that the remainder of the play leads to a second climax in Brutus' downfall and death. Still others suggest that this is a play without a hero, that Shakespeare's point of view was ambiguous, and that he was examining the many aspects of civil insurrection. The decision finally falls into the hands of each reader, for Shakespeare, above all else, was conscious of his audience, an extremely mixed group comprised of members from all levels of social, economic, and intellectual life. His plays communicate with people on all levels because Shakespeare designed them to do just that, and their durability may be directly attributed to the fact that Shakespeare had the genius of ambiguity, the power to suggest different meanings to different men of different times. Perhaps the problems of the climax, the play's hero, and its unity, should be confronted stoically with the thoughts Shakespeare put into the mouth of Cicero: "But men may construe things after their fashion,/ Clean from the purpose of the things themselves" (I. iii).

ACT III: SCENE II

Later on the same day, the ides of March, throngs of citizens crowd the Forum of Rome. They are angry and fearful at Caesar's death.

When Brutus and Cassius arrive, some among them cry, "We will be satisfied! Let us be satisfied!" Brutus divides the crowd so that some stay to hear him speak, while others go off to listen to Cassius. Brutus begins to speak in a dry, emotionless prose. Logically and coldly, he appeals to the wisdom and judgment of the crowd, asking them to trust his honor so that they may believe his reasons. First he addresses "any in this assembly, any dear friend of Caesar's, "to whom Brutus says that his own love for Caesar was no less than his. If then that friend demand why Brutus rose against Caesar, this is the answer: "Not that I loved Caesar less, but that I loved Rome more." He declares that Caesar would have enslaved them if he had lived, and asks them if they would rather be slaves and have Caesar alive or be free men and have Caesar dead. He tells the mob: "As Caesar loved me, I weep for him; as he was fortunate, I rejoice at it; as he was valiant, I honor him, but as he was ambitious, I slew him." He asks any so base as to be a slave to speak up, or any so rude as to be other than a Roman, or any "so vile as will not love his country." Brutus then asserts that the reason for Caesar's death is a matter of official record in the books of the Senate.

As Antony appears with the body of Caesar, Brutus announces that Antony, although he had no part in the slaying, will receive all the benefits of Caesar's death, a place in the commonwealth, as shall all the crowd. Finally, he closes his speech with the words, "As I slew my best lover for the good of Rome, I have the same dagger for myself, when it shall please my country to need my death." Moved by Brutus' oratory, the crowd cries, "Live, Brutus! Live, live!" Some of the citizens suggest that they build a statue of Brutus. Another exclaims, "Let him be Caesar." Brutus silences the mob and asks them all to stay and hear Antony praise Caesar. Before he leaves, be orders that none depart before Antony finishes his speech, save himself.

Comment

Brutus' speech is typical of his own fallacious reasoning. He naively believes that by claiming honor for his name his deed will be accepted as honorable. He feels that by calling Caesar ambitious, he has given clear and cogent reasons for Caesar's death. He believes that the mob will be won over by the simple explanation of his motives, and, indeed, they are. But the mob is not won by any reasoning they have heard; Brutus has flattered them by addressing them as equals, by claiming his concern for their liberty, and by forcing them to deny that they are base, uncultivated, unpatriotic slaves. He has moved the passions of the crowd by his theatrical promise to kill himself if it should please the country, and he hopes to show the mob how noble and just he really is by demanding that Caesar's funeral oration gets a respectful hearing. As for the reasons for Caesar's murder, the mob learns only that Caesar was "ambitious." They are easily persuaded by the tricks of oratory, although Brutus has made a sincere speech which he thinks reasonable. The crowd, however, has missed Brutus' point, for although he has intimated that he has freed them from the bondage of a monarch, shouts are raised that Brutus should be crowned, immortalized by a statue, or be made Caesar himself. They have no idea of the point of the murder and are only aware that Brutus is an honorable and agreeable man who likes Romans and hates ambition.

Antony, however, is not a man of the crowd. He listens carefully as Brutus speaks, finds no satisfaction in Brutus' "reasons," and prepares a shrewd and ironic rebuttal for his funeral speech.

Brutus' naïve political judgment is nowhere more evident than at the moment when he turns the mob over to Antony, when he gives Antony the last word and leaves the scene entirely, foolishly trusting that all will go as he has ordered it without his personal supervision, and foolishly believing that his personal idealism and fallacious reasoning will prevail with Antony as well as with the crowd.

As Antony makes his way to the pulpit, one citizen exclaims, "Twere best he speak no harm of Brutus here," while another cries out, "This Caesar was a tyrant," and another answers, "Nay, that's certain,/ We are blest that Rome is rid of him." Antony mounts the pulpit and begins his speech: "Friends, Romans, countrymen, lend me your ears;/ I come to bury Caesar, not to praise him." Antony declares that the evil which men do lives after them, not their good; "So let it be with Caesar." Pretending thus to agree with Brutus, Antony continues, "The noble Brutus/ Hath told you Caesar was ambitious./ If it were so, it was a grievous fault." (He does not state it was so.) Antony repeats again and again that Brutus has called Caesar ambitious, "and Brutus is an honorable man." The speech continues to relate how Caesar wept when the poor cried out. "Ambition should be made of sterner stuff:/ Yet Brutus says he was ambitious;/ And Brutus is an honorable man." Antony reminds the crowd that Caesar had refused the crown three times at the Lupercal. "Yet Brutus says he was ambitious;/ And sure, he is an honorable man." Antony reminds his listeners that they all loved Caesar once and not without cause. What keeps them from mourning him now, Antony exclaims, crying, "O judgment, thou art fled to brutish beasts,/ And men have lost their reason!" Bursting with emotion, Antony mourns, "My heart is in the coffin there with Caesar,/ And I must pause till it come back to me."

As Antony weeps, the plebeians comment on his remarks. There is reason in them, one plebeian observes. "He would not take the crown; / Therefore 'tis certain he was not ambitious." Another, totally converted to Antony's cause, asserts, "There's not a nobler man in Rome than Antony."

Comment

Antony's skill in verse and dramatic presentation displayed throughout the oration may be attributed to his love for plays and music. These arts were regarded as important aspects in the education of a Renaissance prince or statesman-orator, a value effectively displayed in Antony's verbal victory over the mob.

Antony does not present a direct line of reasoning at first but uses irony, implication, and constant repetition. Hoping to strike home his point that the only proof of Caesar's ambition which Brutus has offered is that Brutus, a man of honor, says that Caesar was ambitious, Antony works the idea of Caesar's ambition and Brutus' honor into every other line. He alternates ironical allusions to Brutus' honor with concrete instances of Caesar's generosity, public concern, and lack of ambition. Then he applies reason to the emotional brew he is concocting. If Caesar was ambitious, why did he refuse the crown three times? The crowd is in no position to consider the question rationally, for they had actually forced him to reject it by cheering his refusals. Instead, they draw the conclusions which Antony desires. To make the dam of public opinion burst, Antony theatrically weeps over Caesar's coffin. He appeals to the sympathy of the crowd, dropping real tears and growing red in the eyes. Many plebeians are moved; one is totally won over, but the speech goes on until every last man in the crowd is a frenzied avenger.

Having composed himself, Antony begins to speak again. He says that he means not to inflame them against the conspirators, for they are all honorable men. Then he produces Caesar's will from his cloak, and holds it up for the people to see. Antony says he cannot read the will, since if he does, "they would go and kiss dead Caesar's wounds,/ And dip their napkins in his sacred blood." A citizen shouts out for Antony to read the will. He refuses again, saying that if he reads the will, they would find out how much Caesar loved them, and the knowledge would inflame them and make them mad. The same citizen cries out again for the will to be read. Antony calls for patience and ironically says that he has gone too far: "I fear I wrong the honorable men/ Whose daggers have stabbed Caesar: I do fear it." Another citizen cries, "They are traitors. Honorable men!" Still another shouts, "They were villains, murderers. The will! Read the will!" Antony finally consents to read the will and tells the crowd to make a ring about Caesar's body so that he can show them him who made the will.

Comment

Part of the crowd had already been won over when Antony paused to weep. Recovering his composure and continuing in an ironic vein, Antony claims that he doesn't want a counter-rebellion, while this is actually his very desire. But Antony draws from a large bag of rhetorical tricks and next produces Caesar's will, which he refuses to read. Thus, he works on the curiosity of the crowd until they are eating out of his hand. When the citizens persist long enough. Antony promises to read but does not do so at once. The reading requires staging to be most effective, Antony knows. The plebeians must gather around the corpse, and they eagerly do so. Thus, the hostile crowd has been subdued and seduced. Brutus' argument for Caesar's killing has been successfully undermined by Antony's insinuations by the time the citizens, like children anxious to hear a story, form a circle around the coffin.

Antony descends from the pulpit and comes down to Caesar's body. He takes Caesar's cloak in his hand and begins to speak. He says that Caesar first put on this cloak on the day he conquered the Gallic tribe, the Nervii. He points to a tear in the cloak and says, "Look in this place ran Cassius' dagger through./ See what a rent the envious Casca made." Then he points to the wound that Brutus made and explains, "Brutus, as you know, was Caesar's angel:/ Judge, O you gods, how dearly Caesar loved him!/ This was the most unkindest cut of all;/ For, when the noble Caesar saw him stab,/ Ingratitude, more strong than traitors' arms,/ Quite vanquish'd him. Then burst his mighty heart,/ And, in his mantle muffling up his face,/ Even at the base of Pompey's statue/ (Which all the while ran blood), great Caesar fell." Then Antony openly calls the bloody deed treason. The crowd is weeping now over Caesar's mutilated clothing, and Antony asks why they weep over mere clothing. "Look you here! Here is himself, marred as you see with traitors." Dramatically, Antony reveals Caesar's corpse to the horror-stricken view of the public.

Comment

Now that Antony knows the crowd is on his side, he proceeds to arouse their wrath against the conspirators. He uses visual aids to illustrate well-known anecdotes. He displays Caesar's cloak, torn by foul wounds, and tells them it was worn against the Nervii to remind the crowd of Caesar's glories. Next Antony makes them visualize the slaughter by describing how the rents in the cloak were made and by naming a conspirator for each hole. The fact that Antony did not witness the murder has no bearing on his oratory. Antony's indictment of the conspirators becomes open at this point, and the plebeians who had warned him not to speak ill of Brutus are now ready to tear Brutus limb from limb. Effectively and completely, Antony has won over the mob, but he is not finished yet. He must direct them to action.

At the point when Antony drops his irony and openly calls the conspirators traitors, the crowd becomes angry and ugly.

The citizens shout, "Revenge! About! Seek! Burn! Fire! Kill! Slay! Let not a traitor live!" But Antony cries halt and, resuming his irony, he says this murder was the deed of honorable men. He adds that he is not an orator like Brutus and that he speaks with the leave of the conspirators, who know very well that Antony has "neither wit, nor words, nor worth,/ Action, nor utterance, nor the power of speech to stir men's blood." He only tells the crowd what they already know and shows Caesar's wounds so they can speak for him. He adds, "But were I Brutus,/ And Brutus Antony, there were an Antony/ Would ruffle up your spirits, and put a tongue/ In every wound of Caesar, that should move/ The stones of Rome to rise and mutiny." The suggestion planted, the citizens shout out, "We'll mutiny." One citizen suggests, "We'll burn the house of Brutus." As the citizens are about to leave the Forum and begin the pillaging of the murderers' houses, Antony calls halt again, for they have forgotten the will which Antony was going to read. Antony then reads: "To every Roman citizen he gives/ To every several man, seventy-five drachmas." A citizen calls out, "Most noble Caesar! We'll revenge his death." Antony continues, "Moreover, he hath left you all his walks,/ His private arbors, and new-planted orchards,/ On this side Tiber; he hath left them you,/ And to your heirs for ever-common pleasures,/ To walk abroad, and recreate yourselves./ Here was a Caesar! When comes such another?"

The citizens are now wild with fury; they pile up benches, tables, and stalls from the Forum to use as fuel for Caesar's funeral pyre, which they plan to erect in a holy place. The crowd leaves with the body of Caesar to bring it to the holy place for cremation. Antony muses to himself over the results of his speech, "Now let it work. Mischief, thou art afoot,/ Take thou what course thou wilt."

Comment

Antony has played the crowd as he might a flute, sounding them and stopping them at will. He has used wit, words, worth, action, utterance, and "the power of speech to stir men's blood" (all the rhetorical tricks which, ironically, he claimed he did not have) to work the crowd into a frenzy of passion, to set mischief afoot, as he remarks in his Machiavellian aside.

A servant enters with a message that Octavius has already arrived in Rome. He and Lepidus are at Caesar's house. Antony replies that he will come at once, that Octavius' arrival is like the granting of a wish. "Fortune is merry," Antony remarks, and so is Antony. The servant reports that he has heard that Brutus and Cassius "are rid like madmen through the gates of Rome." To this, Antony remarks, "Belike they had some notice of the people,/ How I had moved them." Antony and the servant leave for the house of Caesar where Octavius awaits them.

SUMMARY

The first climax of the play having been reached and the action having been pointed in the direction of revenge and civil disorder, as Antony had prophesied, the second scene of Act III works as a transition between the two phases of the plot, the murder and the revenge.

The capriciousness of the mob had been prepared for in the first scene of the play. Thoughtlessly, the mob had turned out to celebrate Caesar's triumph over Pompey, whom they had formerly loved. Now they are moved by Brutus, the betrayer of Caesar, not by reason but out of thoughtless respect for Brutus' honor. Just as rapidly as they turned to Brutus' views, so do they turn to Antony's. But Antony has the shrewd judgment of a practiced orator and public manipulator. He does not let his audience go until they are so enraged that they will not listen to the simplest reason or answer the simplest plea for mercy. Worked to a frenzy by Antony's "mischief," the mob goes off crying "havoc." Antony's prophesy over the body of Caesar has moved toward fulfillment, and the plebeians' irrational behavior in the next scene has been prepared for amply.

The two speeches given in this scene are designed to contrast their speakers and their oratorical styles. Brutus' speech, in prose, is terse, emotionless; it appeals to the cool judgment of men, although its reasoning is questionable. Antony's speech, in verse, is emotional, lengthy, dramatic; it makes use of wit, repetition, action, visual effects. Antony makes his listeners participate in the development of his argument by pausing frequently to give them time to react, by drawing them into a circle around Caesar's body, by making them recall a famous victory in which, as Romans, they had shared Caesar's glory.

A new, powerful side of Antony's character is revealed in this scene. This is a far shrewder Antony than we have seen before, when he followed at the heels of Caesar, a well-fed, sleek-headed fellow, given to pleasures. Then he was simply a man to be trusted, but his taste for the arts suggested his nobler parts; now his loyalty in friendship, his skill in oratory, his ability to know men (perhaps learned from Caesar) come to the fore.

Brums is seen in the first stages of his decline. His faulty reasoning and his poor judgment of men combine with his overconfidence in the virtues of reason and lofty idealism and make him reject the minor vices which must be practiced in persuasive oratory. His prose reflects his dry, rational approach to life and contrasts sharply with Antony's musical verse, his use of dramatic effects, and his appeals to emotion.

Caesar or the spirit of Caesar is the subject of both orations. From Brutus's point of view, we hear that Caesar was ambitious; from Antony's that he was glorious, victorious, tender, generous. Caesar speaks to the people once more when Antony reads his will aloud. Although dead in body, Caesar's spirit remains, and his shrewd political judgment is revealed in his final bequest. The good that Caesar does will live after him in the gift of money, parks, and pleasures that he bequeaths the people.

At the close of the scene, the meeting of Antony, Lepidus, and Octavius hints at the force which is mustering to destroy the conspirators and prepares us for the action of Acts IV and V.

ACT III: SCENE III

Later that day on the ides of March, Cinna the poet is seen on a street near the Forum. As he walks along, he muses over a dream he has had in which he feasted with Caesar. Now omens of evil are charging his imagination. He does not wish to go out of doors, but something leads him forward. A band of citizens suddenly appears and questions Cinna; asking his name, where he is going, where he lives, and if he is married or a bachelor. Wittily, Cinna replies that he is "wisely ... a bachelor." An enraged citizen interprets this as an insult to married men and promises to beat Cinna for calling him a fool. Cinna then reports that he is going to Caesar's funeral as a friend. When he answers that his name is Cinna, one citizen cries that he is a conspirator: "Tear him to pieces!" Cinna protests that he is Cinna the poet, not Cinna the conspirator. But another citizen, completely unreasonable, shouts, "Tear him for his bad verses!" When Cinna again pleads that he is the poet, still another plebeian answers, "It is no matter, his name's Cinna! Pluck but his name out of his heart, and turn him going." Madly they set upon the helpless poet, and when they have finished rending him, they charge off to burn the houses of Brutus, Cassius, Decius, and the rest.

Comment and Summary

Cinna was a distinguished poet, a close friend of Caesar, and a tribune of the people. He is not portrayed here in his historical personage but as the Elizabethan stereotype of the court poet of ancient Rome. Poets, it was held among the ancients, had powers of prophecy and the ability to envision the future in their imaginations. Cinna the poet, musing over his ominous dream, shows these legendary powers.

The ancient poet was also a satirist of the people and his times. Cinna in this scene indulges in some trivial foolery over the wisdom of remaining a bachelor, a familiar jest both in ancient times and in our own.

The crowd is in no humor to be amused, and Cinna's wit is taken as an insult to married men. Even so, no reason is necessary to turn the inflamed mob against the first victim they find in the streets. Antony had promised Caesar revenge and a quota of horrible slaughter, which the plebeians are now prepared to take. The spirit of the mob, created in the preceding scene, is dramatized in the tearing of Cinna. In addition, Cinna's ominous dream introduces the theme of murder, just as Calpurnia's dream anticipated Caesar's slaughter. Omens will continue to be used as forecasts of death and destruction for the remainder of the play.

JULIUS CAESAR

ACT IV

ACT IV: SCENE I

The scene now shifts to a room in Antony's house where Antony, Octavius, and Lepidus are holding council. They are found in the middle of their discussion, deciding who is to be killed in the reign of terror which they are about to begin. Octavius tells Lepidus, "Your brother too must die. Consent you, Lepidus?" Lepidus consents "upon condition that Publius shall not live,/ Who is your sister's son, Mark Antony." Antony calmly agrees to this. Antony then sends Lepidus to Caesar's house to fetch Caesar's will in order to see if they can eliminate some of the heirs.

Comment

The meeting of the Caesarist party parallels the earlier meeting held by Brutus' faction. Here as there, an elimination list has been proposed; it is being decided who may be hostile to the party and must die because of it. Unlike Brutus, Antony is calmly prepared to execute his enemies, even his own sister's son, Publius.

(Historically, it was Lucius Caesar, Antony's uncle, who was marked for death in this way. Shakespeare's distortion of this historical fact serves the special purpose of emphasizing the inhumanity and villainy which insurrection fosters. By making Antony condemn his own nephew, Shakespeare shows the cruelty of which Antony is capable, for in ancient Rome, a sister's son was generally raised and adopted by men of repute and often became the heirs of their uncle's great estates. Hence, Antony's consent to Publius' death is as unnatural as a father's execution of his own son.)

Share w/ the class

In view of Antony's Machiavellian behavior, the deals he makes over the lives of Lepidus' brother and his own nephew calls Antony's honor into question, and his ironic regard for Brutus who "is an honorable man" begins to suggest this double irony that Brutus is really honorable, and that Antony does think so, although he pretends not to for the political purpose of rabble-rousing.

✱flip the page!

As Lepidus leaves, Antony tells Octavius that Lepidus has little merit as a man and is only fit to do errands. He asks if it is right that this man should get a third part of the world. Octavius answers that Antony seemed to think well of Lepidus when he asked his advice about the proscription lists. But Antony replies he has been using Lepidus as a scapegoat on whom the blame for the murders may be placed later on. Lepidus follows where they lead, or leads where they tell him to go. He will be discarded like an ass set to pasture when it has delivered its burden. Octavius leaves these plans up to Antony, but interjects that Lepidus is a

→ Condemnation = condemned

tried and valiant soldier. Antony insists once more that Lepidus can only be regarded as property like a horse. Then he reports that Brutus and Cassius are beginning to gather their forces and that now is the time for unity and for taking council. Octavius assents and they leave to make plans.

Comment

The meeting of Antony's party, which has been taken up at mid-point, is to be understood as the one in which the second triumvirate was formed. That is, the three men were to govern Rome with the advice of the Senate.

Antony's machine-like mind continues to be portrayed in his feelings over Lepidus. He shows how little he values men, even those whose service has been courageous and loyal. He believes in using men as he uses animals to serve his own ambitions and needs.

In contrast to Brutus' meeting with the conspirators earlier in the play, Antony has his cohorts well in hand. When suggestions are raised, he yields and consents to them. There are no half-way measures for the practical ruler. At the same time, Lepidus agrees fully to Antony's proposals, and Octavius accedes to Antony's plan to discard Lepidus even though he regards him as a tried and valiant soldier. However brutal the triumvirate may seem, there is far more unity and promise of success in their alliance than was seen among Brutus' conspirators.

SUMMARY

In this scene, Antony is revealed as a cruel, conniving and ambitious man, an opportunist who will seize the first

Isn't this why Caesar was Killed?

chance he gets to gain full control over Rome. The cruelty of the entire triumvirate is manifest in the ambitious nature of each of its members, and their plan to attack Brutus and Cassius is motivated as much out of the desire for power as for revenge. Thus, Antony, once the friend and pupil of Caesar, is now seen in the light of his unscrupulous ambition; Octavius who is docile for the moment is shown as the willing accomplice in the quest for power; Lepidus who goes off on his errand like the mule Antony calls him promises to be little competition to the two dominant members of the triumvirate. Caesar's ambition, the spirit of Caesarism, lives on in these two.

The triumvirate's council works as a contrast and balance to the meeting of the conspirators in Brutus' garden. The differences to be noted are that Antony shows the powers of calculation which Cassius has, but he has the power to influence his cohorts which Cassius does not have. Octavius takes things at face value as Brutus does, but he is acquiescent to the political wisdom of the acknowledged leader of the triumvirate.

Two new characters are introduced in this scene as complements to Antony and as a balance and contrast to Brutus' team. Antony's cool nature resembles that of Cassius; Octavius' naiveté is balanced by Brutus'; and Lepidus' fatuity parallels Casca's.

ACT IV: SCENE II

The scene now shifts to a camp near Sardis where Brutus' army has pitched its tents. Drums are sounded as Brutus arrives before his tent accompanied by Lucilius, Titinius, and other soldiers. Lucius, Brutus' servant, is also present. Lucilius has just returned from a visit to Cassius' camp, accompanied by Pindarus. Brutus tells Pindarus that his master Cassius has given him some cause to wish "things done, undone." Pindarus replies that his master will appear "such as he is, full of regard and honor." Brutus then asks Lucilius how he was received by Cassius, and Lucilius explains that he was received with courtesy and respect, but not with the old familiarity that Cassius used to show. Brutus tells Lucilius that he has witnessed a "hot friend cooling," and he compares Cassius to a horse which seems spirited at the start but quickly falls under trial of battle. He then learns from Lucilius that Cassius' army will be camping at Sardis that night.

Comment

Attention is shifted from the triumvirate planning its action against Brutus to Brutus' camp, where the insurgents are preparing to fight Antony's forces. Servants arrive to report Cassius' arrival and information is exchanged which suggests that discord between Cassius and Brutus has grown since our last view of them. Brutus' feelings toward Cassius are expressed when he compares his ally to a horse, hot at the start, unreliable in the finish, and the comparison works as a link to the previous scene in which Antony compared Lepidus to a horse and as a **foreshadowing** of subsequent events in which Cassius will prove unreliable in battle, quick to admit complete defeat, and overly hasty in suicide. Such figures of language force comparisons to be made, work as binding elements among the scenes, and supply much of the unity of the play, which is often difficult to see on the surface. It is intended next that the conflict between the Republican conspirators be compared and contrasted with the momentary harmony of the triumvirate.

Cassius enters with several soldiers and greets Brutus with the words, "Most noble brother, you have done me wrong." He accuses Brutus of hiding his wrongs under "this sober form of yours." Brutus reminds Cassius of his hasty temper and tells him not to wrangle in front of their two armies. Both armies are led off some distance as Brutus and Cassius enter the tent where Brutus regally promises, "I will give you audience."

Comment and Summary

The argument which ensues in the next scene is anticipated by Cassius' greeting to Brutus and his charge that Brutus hides his wrongs under the appearance of virtue. Cassius has changed since his last appearance; his irascible behavior during the subsequent argument is predicted when Brutus alludes to Cassius' rash temper and urges Cassius not to speak before their men. Brutus is seen to be in control of the situation; he is more confident and self-assured than ever, but his political naiveté shows no improvement here or in the subsequent scene. This hint of discord between the conspirators will be confirmed and the suggestion of defeat, which accompanies discord, will prevail from this point on.

ACT IV: SCENE III

Inside the tent, Cassius tells Brutus he has been wronged because Brutus has condemned Lucius Pella for taking bribes from the Sardians, even after Cassius had sent letters entreating him not to dismiss Pella. Cassius adds that this is not the time to scrutinize and rigidly censure every petty or trifling offense. Brutus reproaches Cassius for selling offices to undeserving men for gold. At this, Cassius becomes infuriated and says that if anyone but Brutus had told him this, he would have been killed on the spot. Speaking of corruption, Brutus says that Cassius himself has set the example among his men and has escaped punishment only because of his high position. Brutus reminds Cassius of the ides of March, how they had struck down Caesar, the foremost man of all the world, for the sake of justice. He asks if they should now "contaminate our fingers with base bribes." Brutus argues, "I had rather be a dog, and bay the moon,/ Than such a Roman." "Brutus, bait not me;/ I'll not endure it," Cassius warns. He adds that Brutus forgets himself when he attempts to restrain Cassius' actions, for Cassius is a more experienced soldier and more able "to make conditions," that is to make bargains with men and officers. Indignantly, Brutus retorts that Cassius is not more able; Cassius insists he is; Brutus contradicts. Cassius warns Brutus to provoke him no farther, but Brutus insists that Cassius had better listen, since he will not be silenced by Cassius' rash temper. When he asserts that he cannot be frightened by a madman, Cassius exclaims, "O ye gods, ye gods! Must I endure all this?" Viciously, Brutus warns Cassius that he will defy him until "you shall digest the venom of your spleen," and he promises that Cassius will be the object of his ridicule from this day forth. Sarcastically, Brutus urges Cassius to prove he is a "better soldier," for he is anxious to learn from "noble men." Cassius protests, "I said, an elder soldier, not a better." He asserts that Caesar dared not treat him so, and Brutus replies that Cassius had not dared to provoke him as he dares Brutus now. Now at the peak of his anger, Cassius threatens, "Do not presume too much upon my love;/ I may do that I shall be sorry for." Brutus replies arrogantly that Cassius has already done what he should be sorry for and that his threats have no terror for Brutus, "for I am arm'd so strong in honesty/ That they pass by me as the idle wind." Next Brutus complains that Cassius did not send him any of the gold which he had badly needed, for he cannot raise money by vile means, that is, by extorting it from local peasants. Cassius claims that he did not deny Brutus the gold but that the messenger who delivered his reply was a fool. Cassius charges that Brutus no longer loves him, for he refuses to tolerate Cassius' weaknesses and makes them even greater than they are. Cassius unsheathes his dagger, and, handing it to Brutus, he says, "I, that denied thee gold, will give my heart:/ Strike, as thou didst at Caesar, for, I know,/ When thou didst hate him worst, thou lovedst him better/ Than ever thou lovedst Cassius."

Comment

During the entire argument, Brutus shows that he is still incapable of managing men. He is too truthful, too "sober," too noble to resort to practical necessities of war. He has become arrogant and overconfident, on the one hand, denying Cassius' superiority as a soldier and as a raiser of funds, and on the other hand admitting that he is unable to raise his own money, which he regards not as a soldierly weakness but as a sign of his noble nature. Cassius' methods of appointing officers and raising money are corrupt but practical. The incorruptible Brutus, however, will not engage in practical immorality.

The argument of the two men follows the childish pattern of insistence, denial, insistence, denial. "You did," "I didn't," children might say. The heroic assassins of the mighty Caesar behave like children who have lost a tyrannical father and unconsciously suggest that Caesar, at least, had maintained harmony among these children. The irrational argument, furthermore, displays both men in a state of angry madness, which, the ancients believed, was inflicted upon men whom the gods would destroy.

The pride Brutus takes in his unassailable honesty is reminiscent of Caesar's pride in his unassailable constancy just before he was killed and presages the imminent destruction of Brutus himself. Brutus taunts Cassius with his own virtuous honesty and his immunity to threats: "I am arm'd so strong in honesty," etc. To the audience, the effect is shocking; to Cassius, it is maddening. Pressed to his limit, Cassius bares his breast and, like Caesar, is prepared to die because he has lost Brutus' love. The harshness Brutus had displayed in his ability to subordinate his personal feelings to his ideal of good in the slaying of Caesar is reasserted in his cruel abuse of his friend Cassius.

This famous Quarrel Scene is one of the best exhibits in Shakespeare of his knowledge of human nature; it has won the praise and interest of critics through the ages and has moved even those who did not like *Julius Caesar* as a whole.

Seeing Cassius with his bosom bared and his dagger offered for his death, Brutus apologetically tells Cassius to sheathe his dagger and "be angry when you will." Brutus compares himself to a lamb that carries anger only briefly as a flint afire one moment is cold the next. Brutus is sorry he has laughed at Cassius' weakness of temperament, promises to tolerate it in the future, and the friends are reconciled.

Suddenly, there is a disturbance outside the door. A poet is trying to gain admittance to the tent on the grounds that he must stop the quarrel within, for the two generals should not be alone at such a time. Lucilius, who has been guarding the entry, refuses to admit the poet, but the poet insists, "Nothing but death shall stay me." Cassius appears and inquires the poet's errand and learns, through some doggerel verses, that someone who is older than either of the generals knows it is not fitting for them to fight. Cassius laughs at the poet and at the inferior quality of the rhymes, but Brutus is annoyed and says that foolish poets are out of place in war. Although Cassius is tolerant of the new fashion of taking poets to war, Brutus orders the poet to be gone. Then Brutus orders Lucilius and Titinius to bid the officers to make camp for the night, and Cassius adds that Messala is to be brought to them immediately.

Comment

The reconciliation having been effected when both parties admit they have been ill-tempered, the tension is released by the poet who bursts in and anti-climactically attempts to effect the reconciliation which has already been made. The poet's exaggerated vow to enter the general's tent or die is funny in itself, and his doggerel verses add to the comedy of the moment. However, the gist of the verses suggests the childishness which has been displayed during the quarrel, for the poet affects a kind of paternal authority over the disputants by claiming to "have seen more years" than they.

Cassius' response to the poet is characteristic. Although we have been told that Cassius rarely smiles, we have also learned that when he does, he smiles as if in self-mockery. The poet, whom Cassius calls a cynic (one who satirizes men), has enabled Cassius to smile at himself. Brutus, however, is a Stoic of sorts, who has never been "gamesome." Here he shows his complete lack of humor and his priggish sense of decorum when he orders the "saucy fellow, hence."

The poet gone, Brutus asks Lucius, his servant, for a bowl of wine. Cassius remarks that he did not think it was possible to make Brutus so angry. But Brutus explains that he hears many griefs. Cassius reminds Brutus to make use of his philosophy in facing evil events. Then calmly Brutus tells Cassius that Portia is dead. Amazed at this news, Cassius wonders how Brutus prevented himself from killing Cassius when he had crossed him so. He asks of what sickness Portia had died. Brutus replies that, impatient of his absence and seeing Mark Antony and Octavius grow strong, she killed herself by swallowing fire. Appalled, Cassius cries, "O ye immortal gods!

Comment

The philosophy to which Cassius refers is Stoicism, a creed by which men accepted human events with resignation and quietude. Brutus' uncharacteristic anger is thus explained as the diversion of his grief over Portia's death. This is the first sign that Brutus is in a state of mental deterioration. Soon he will see spirits, which is how Shakespeare commonly dramatized the condition of the unhealthy mind.

Lucius reenters with wine and tapers. Brutus says he buries all unkindness in a bowl of wine, while Cassius says, "I cannot drink too much of Brutus' love." Titinius and Messala arrive and are told that Brutus has received letters saying that Octavius and Antony are marching with a mighty force toward Philippi. Messala says he has had letters to the same effect and adds that Octavius, Antony, and Lepidus have murdered a hundred senators. Brutus remarks that their letters differ in this point, since his report says seventy senators had been killed, Cicero among them. Messala asks if Brutus has received any news from his wife. Brutus replies he has not and asks Messala if he has heard anything. Messala reports that Portia is dead. Brutus, with philosophic quietude, states, "With meditating that she must die once,/ I have the patience to endure it now."

Messala compliments Brutus on his stoical acceptance of Portia's death; this is the way great men should endure their losses, he says. Cassius states that he knows as much about the theory of Stoicism as Brutus does, but his nature (rash and choleric) could not bear grief with the resistance of the Stoic.

Comment

The discrepancy in the reports over the number of Senators killed by Antony is a realistic device frequently used by Shakespeare to suggest the confused nature of things during time of war and to introduce the **theme** of false report which later will be so vital to the tragedy of Cassius.

Brutus allows Messala to tell him Portia has died, although he has already heard this news. We have been shown that messages delivered over long distances are often unreliable and contradictory. Brutus realizes this when he patiently listens for confirmation of Portia's death. When the first report is confirmed by the second, Brutus' response is, "Why farewell, Portia." This may be taken to mean that Brutus was reluctant to bid farewell until he was absolutely certain of her death.

Other explanations have been offered for the double report of Portia's death. One attributes it to the carelessness of the compositor, who failed to remove the second report, which was marked for deletion. Another, within the context of the play, claims it to be the consideration of Brutus, who lets Messala deliver his report out of respect for his office.

Brutus' reaction to Portia's death is reminiscent of Caesar's belief that "the valiant never taste of death but once." A comparison is forced upon the reader who recalls the verbal and philosophic resemblances between Caesar's statement and Brutus' stoical idea that Portia "must die once." As Messala observes, this stoical resignation to death is the mark of a great man. Cassius, purportedly an Epicurean at this point in the play, admits that he is unable to bear grief like a Stoic, suggesting that he is not a great man. However, he will shortly renounce his Epicurean philosophy and die a Stoic. The implication is that Cassius' character becomes ennobled as the play progresses.

Anxious to leave the subject of Portia's death, Brutus suggests that they march to Philippi with their armies, but Cassius is against this plan. He feels it is better to let the enemy come to them, wearying their troops in the long march, while Brutus and Cassius' men are rested and ready to defend themselves. Brutus counters Cassius' suggestion by asserting that the enemy will gather fresh troops along the way among the people Brutus and Cassius have antagonized by extorting their money. Silencing Cassius, Brutus argues further that the morale of their troops is at its highest, and that if they wait, the morale will decrease. Cassius reluctantly agrees to march to Philippi. Brutus announces that it is time for rest, and Cassius begs Brutus that such a disagreement as had begun that night may never again come between their souls. Brutus replies, "Everything is well," and as Cassius, Titinius, and Messala leave, each in turn addresses him as "my lord" or "Lord Brutus."

Comment

Brutus' will has been asserted among his allies, who are forced to accept his decision to march against the enemy rather than wait for the enemy to attack. Cassius offers some feeble opposition to this plan, but, anxious to prevent any further discord, he quickly concedes to the stronger man. By the time the council is over, Cassius acknowledges Brutus as "my lord," as do Titinius and Messala. Thus, Brutus' poor judgment in military affairs prevails over the sounder advice of Cassius, the more experienced soldier, and draws closer the tragic end that awaits the two men.

Preparing for rest, Brutus calls for his gown and asks Lucius to find his instrument (lute). Paternally, he notes that Lucius is drowsy from having served all day. He sends for Varro and Claudius to sleep in his tent in the event that messengers to Cassius are needed during the night. The two soldiers offer to stand guard all night, but Brutus considerately insists that they sleep until they are called. From the pocket of his gown, Brutus produces a book he had blamed Lucius for misplacing and apologizes to his servant for being so forgetful. Still apologetic, Brutus asks the tired boy to play a tune and promises to reward him if Brutus lives. Music and a song follow before Lucius falls asleep. Tenderly, Brutus removes the lute from Lucius' hands. Then, finding his book, Brutus begins to read.

Comment

Brutus' obstinate will and his poor military judgment give way to another side of the man. Here he is considerate of his men, who, in return, serve him loyally. To Lucius, his young servant, he is paternal and tender, and his promise to be good to Lucius if he lives is unquestionably a sincere one. The qualification to the promise, however, introduces a new idea. There is doubt in Brutus' mind and, perhaps, fear of death. The contrast between Brutus' treatment of his men and Antony's attitude toward Lepidus may be noted at this point.

As Brutus picks up his book to read, the ghost of Caesar, unnoticed by Brutus, appears in the tent. Brutus observes that the taper burns poorly. Then, suddenly, he sees the apparition, which he tries to attribute to the weakness of his eyes. As the spirit draws closer, Brutus asks, "Art thou some god, some angel, or some devil,/ That mak'st my blood cold and my hair to stare?"/ Speak to me what thou art."

The ghost answers, "Thy evil spirit, Brutus." Brutus asks why the spirit has come, to which the ghost replies, "To tell thee that thou shalt see me at Philippi." Then I shall see you again, Brutus asks? "Ay, at Philippi," the ghost replies. The ghost disappears as suddenly as it has come. "Now that I have taken heart, thou vanishest," Brutus exclaims.

Comment

The taper flickers; Brutus is not certain what he sees, but he is frightened by the apparition, whatever it may be. His blood runs cold, his hair stands on end. The question of whether or not the spirit is an angel or devil reflects the divided opinion held during the Renaissance on the existence and the nature of ghosts. Physicians and realists of the age attributed apparitions to an excess of the melancholic humor or the "melancholy adust," produced under the influence of a hot passion like anger. Others who believed in the supernatural thought that ghosts were spirits of the dead released from purgatory. Some thought they were good angels sent by God; still others that they were evil angels sent by Satan.

The fact that the ghost speaks should not be taken as proof that it has objective existence. It may simply be a superstitious projection of Brutus' mind, which has recently been heated by a passionate anger against Cassius and turned melancholy by grief over the death of Portia. Brutus himself admits that his mind has been disordered of late when he apologizes to Lucius for forgetting the book, and he seems to be in doubt over whether or not he will live. (The book, incidentally, is another **anachronism**; Romans used scrolls.) Caesar too had become superstitious in his declining days. The appearance of ghosts and the occurrence of supernatural events is repeatedly associated in Shakespeare with diseases of the mind, sometimes accompanied by somatic disabilities, as in Caesar.

That the ghost tells Brutus he is his "evil spirit" may be taken as a **foreshadowing** of the tragedy at Philippi; it is also a reflection of Brutus' subconscious misgivings over the death of Caesar and his present venture, which Brutus may consciously be incapable of acknowledging. Those in Shakespeare's audience who regarded the ghost as an objective spirit would have seen that supernatural forces were united to the natural ones of Antony to work against Brutus for Caesar's revenge.

In either case the spirit of Caesar, whether real or imagined, has come to plague Brutus. The effect of the ghost is the same; Brutus is frightened, and the death he fears is foreshadowed by the ghost. When Brutus exclaims that the ghost vanishes "now that I have taken heart," the balance swings in favor of a subjective ghost, which is conjured up in the imagination of a troubled mind and disappears when Brutus pulls himself together.

Brutus wakes Lucius, Claudius, and Varro. Lucius, dreaming he is still playing, says, "The strings, my lord, are false." Brutus asks him if he had dreamed and cried out in his sleep, but Lucius says he did not know he cried out and that he saw nothing in the tent. Brutus asks the same questions of Varro and Claudius, and their replies are as negative as Lucius'. Immediately, Brutus sends Varro and Claudius to tell Cassius to set out with his forces promptly and that Brutus will follow close behind.

Comment

Brutus' first reaction to the ghost is to find out whether it was real or imagined. He questions his men to see if any of them spoke in his sleep or saw anything. Since they have perceived nothing, Brutus may suspect that the ghost is a figment of his disturbed imagination, or he may believe that the ghost has made its appearance only to him, as was reportedly the case in a good deal of Renaissance demonology.

Brutus' decision to go to Philippi at once may be explained as characteristic of the behavior which Brutus has revealed earlier in the play during his inner struggle before the murder of Caesar (II.i). At that time, the anticipation of action against Caesar had made him sleepless, and his mind in turmoil was described by Brutus himself as a kind of nightmare, a state of insurrection: "Between the acting of a dreadful thing/ And the first motion, all the interim is/ Like a phantasma or a hideous dream./ The genius and the mortal instruments/ Are then in council, and the state of man,/ Like to a little kingdom, suffers then/ The nature of an insurrection." Now, in IV. iii, Brutus has decided to march to Philippi. Having made the decision to do so, he must await the time of action; but for Brutus this is a time of nightmare, a time of mental insurrection. Brutus is anxious to get to Philippi. His troubled mind seems to conjure up a nightmare, a ghost who will appear at Philippi. When he rouses from his vision or visitation, he orders Cassius to march at once, because, whether he realizes it or not, Brutus cannot bear the state of suspense "between the acting of a dreadful thing,/ And the first motion ...."

SUMMARY

This lengthy scene, which takes place in the rebel camp, may be divided into four stages. In the first stage, Brutus and Cassius engage in a heated argument which stems from the essential differences between the two friends; Brutus' stoical virtue and incorruptible idealism is opposed to Cassius' cynical and practical militarism. The quarrel, however, turns into a childish battle of wills over who is the better man and ends with the total capitulation of Cassius to Brutus, who has shown the stronger will. The theme of discord among the assassins is intended as a contrast to the cold-blooded harmony of the newly-formed triumvirate, which is masterminded by Antony. Brutus' character, during the argument, shows several unfortunate changes. He has become petty and arrogant, self-confident and obstinate in asserting his misguided judgments on his cohorts. Cassius has become a rash, fearful, and beaten man. By the end of the argument, the man who loved freedom so much calls Brutus "my lord."

The second stage of the scene deals with the reconciliation of the quarrelers and the double disclosure that Portia is dead. Cassius now interprets Brutus' anger as having stemmed from grief over Portia, but Brutus is a Stoic, who remains unaffected by the external events of life, and he seems to accept his loss with resignation, as becomes a great man.

The third state of the scene concerns the decision to attack the enemy at Philippi. Cassius' sensible opposition to Brutus' plan is feeble, and it is quickly dropped when it seems that dissension may be renewed between himself and Brutus, whom he loves.

The fourth stage of the scene is marked by the appearance of Caesar's ghost, which Elizabethans interpreted variously as an objective or subjective spirit, angelic or diabolic, or simply as the spirit of the dead risen from purgatory. The ghost vanishes when Brutus' courage returns, so that it seems to be a projection of his troubled mind, heated from the argument with Cassius, depressed by the news of Portia's death, and fearful of the outcome of the battle of Philippi. Rather than endure the nightmare of a delayed departure, Brutus orders Cassius to march at once toward Philippi, and he himself prepares to follow shortly to meet his destiny.

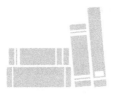

JULIUS CAESAR

ACT V

. . . .

ACT V: SCENE I

The action now shifts to the plains of Philippi where Antony. Octavius, and their armies are encamped. Octavius tells Antony, that their prayers are answered since the enemy is coming to meet them on the plains rather than keep to the hills as Antony had imagined. Antony replies that he knows why the conspirators do this. They are trying to make a show of courage, which Antony does not believe they really have. A messenger enters to announce the enemy's approach. Antony tells Octavius to take the left side of the field, but Octavius demands the right. Antony asks, "Why do you cross me in this exigent?" Octavius ominously replies, "I do not cross you; but I will do so."

Comment

Antony's tone is marked with confidence here; he gives orders to Octavius who is technically his peer, and Octavius shows signs of balking at Antony's command. He demands the right side when ordered to the left and concedes with an ominous warning that while he does not cross Antony now, he will do so in the future. (See Shakespeare's *Antony and Cleopatra*, where the central conflict concerns Octavius' pursuit and victory over Antony.)

The fact that Brutus has forsaken his vantage point in the hills to fight the enemy on the plains is another mark of his poor military judgment and a foreboding of his defeat.

At the sound of drum, Brutus and Cassius lead their army to the field. Lucilius, Titinius, and Messala join them. Brutus notes that Antony and Octavius stand as if to invite a parley. Antony, observing the same hesitation on Brutus' part, decides to answer the enemy's charges before doing battle. Cassius and Brutus advance to meet Antony and Octavius, while the armies wait for a signal from their generals to begin the fray. The rivals exchange insults over Brutus' love of good words and Octavius' penchant for giving bad strokes (in fighting). A master of the discourteous retort, Antony tells Brutus, "In your bad strokes, Brutus, you give good words;/ Witness the hole you made in Caesar's heart,/ Crying 'Long live! Hail, Caesar!'" Antony gets as good as he gives when Cassius reminds him that Antony is yet untried in battle, although his speech is gifted and his honeyed words rob the bees of Mount Hybla. Parrying Cassius' thrust neatly, Antony replies, "Not stingless too." Antony becomes angry as the insults continue, and his taunts become more venomous. "Villains!" he cries. "You did not waste words when your daggers struck Caesar while some of you smiled like apes, fawned like hounds, bowed like bondmen, kissing Caesar's feet, while damned Casca"... stabbed him in the back. "O you flatterers!"

Failing an answer, Cassius turns to Brutus, arguing that if his advice had been followed instead of Brutus', they would not now be listening to Antony's abuses. Octavius draws his sword and swears that he will not sheathe it, "Never, till Caesar's three-and-thirty wounds/ Be well aveng'd; or till another Caesar/ Have added slaughter to the sword of traitors." Brutus replies that Octavius cannot die by traitors' hands unless he himself brought those hands with him. When Octavius says that he was not born to die on Brutus' sword, Brutus replies that he could not die more honorably if he were the noblest of his strain, that is, if he were his uncle, Julius Caesar. In a final insult, Octavius bids Cassius and Brutus to come to the field if they dare to fight that day; if not, they may come when they have the stomachs for a fight.

Comment

This verbal battle in which the rival generals engage before entering physical combat was a medieval rather than a Roman practice, but it serves an important function in this scene, which overrides any annoyance the **anachronism** may cause. It establishes the animosity between the two armies and substitutes verbal combat for physical combat which is difficult to enact on-stage. The generals' abusive wit, moreover, was a source of delight to the Elizabethan audience, which regarded the clever insult as a form of art.

Cassius shows that he still resents Brutus for rejecting his battle plan; Antony and Octavius make it clear that they plan to avenge Caesar, and Brutus still insists on the merits of Caesar's murder.

As Antony, Octavius, and their armies leave the field, Brutus and Lucilius, his lieutenant, go aside to talk, while Cassius and Messala confer in the foreground (downstage). Cassius says that this day is his birthday, and he calls Messala to witness that he is compelled, against his will, to risk everything on one battle, just as Pompey was. Cassius confides that although he had formerly believed in Epicurus, he has now changed his mind and believes, to some extent, in portents and omens. He relates how, on their way from Sardis, two eagles swooped down, ate from the hands of the soldiers, and followed them all the way to Philippi. Now, however, the eagles have flown away, and in their stead, ravens, crows, and kites look down upon them as if they were sickly prey. Advised not to believe in the omen, Cassius admits that he only partly believes in it, for at the same time, he is "fresh of spirit and resolved/ To meet all perils very constantly."

Comment

At the battle of Pharsalia (48 B.C.), Pompey was persuaded against his will to fight Caesar and was decisively defeated. Cassius feels that, like Pompey, he is being forced by Brutus to stake everything on one poorly planned battle and that he too will be defeated by a Caesar, that is, Octavius Caesar.

Cassius explains that he had formerly believed strongly in the philosophy of Epicurus (a materialist who believed that the gods did not interfere in human events so that omens were to be ignored). Now, however, his deep forebodings of doom in the coming battle have led him to discard his former philosophy. On the other hand, although he senses his forthcoming defeat, he is "fresh of spirit and resolved/ To meet all perils," that is, he has purged his mind of fear and anxiety and has apparently taken the Stoic position of resignation to one's fate. In his conversation with Brutus, which follows, Cassius remarks that "the gods today stand friendly," indicating that he does, indeed, believe that gods concern themselves with human events.

Brutus and Cassius finish their conversations with their respective lieutenants and rejoin each other. Cassius suggests that although the gods are favorable, he and Brutus might hold a final conversation before battle. If the worst befalls them, this conversation will be their last, Cassius states; therefore, he asks Brutus what he proposes to do should they lose the day. Brutus replies that he would arm himself with patience and live by the same rule of philosophy he had followed when he had condemned Cato for his "cowardly and vile" suicide. Cassius asks if this means Brutus would be content to be led captive through the streets of Rome, and Brutus arrogantly replies, "No, Cassius, no. Think not, thou noble Roman,/ That ever Brutus will go bound to Rome./ He bears too great a mind." Without revealing how he could escape humiliation and still avoid suicide should he be defeated and taken prisoner, Brutus asserts, "But this same day/ Must end that work the ides of March begun." He bids a final farewell to Cassius and the two part friends. As they go off to battle, Brutus impatiently wishes, "O that a man might know/ The end of this day's business ere it come!"

Comment

Cato, Portia's father, committed suicide at the battle of Utica (46 B.C.) rather than fall into Caesar's hands. In Stoic doctrine, which Brutus presumably follows, suicide in the interest of the public good was condoned. The philosophic principle which Brutus lives by and which holds that suicide is a transgression against the high powers that govern men's lives is really a Platonic (and Christian) one. According to Shakespeare, Brutus has combined Platonism with Stoicism to form his philosophy.

Cassius tries to make Brutus realize that the alternative to death is to be led through the streets of Rome in triumph, but Brutus asserts that he will never face this indignity. At the moment, he is not contemplating suicide, which he regards as "cowardly and vile." He believes that the Fates will pass final judgment at the battle of Philippi for the work that was begun on the ides of March. On that day, just after the assassination, Brutus had called upon the goddesses of destiny: "Fates, we will know your pleasure./ That we shall die, we know, 'tis but the time,/ And drawing days out, that men stand upon." Convinced that the Fates will grant him victory or death, Brutus refuses to face the possibility of defeat and capture, which would force him to choose between humiliation and the betrayal of his philosophic idealism.

The talk of suicide and of parting forever reflects the general pessimism the two men feel and foreshadows both their deaths by suicide. Each man faces possible defeat with characteristic resolution. Cassius, practical and realistic, gives up his former philosophy and embraces a form of Stoicism. He is prepared to commit suicide rather than be taken captive. Brutus still impractical, unrealistic, immutably idealistic, refuses to face the real possibility of defeat without death. Ironically, Brutus will betray the principles he holds so strongly when he commits suicide at last, but he will be honored, nevertheless. Cassius will be honored somewhat less, but his expedient change of creeds before his death allows him to maintain his integrity and die by the principles he has newly embraced.

SUMMARY

This scene juxtaposes the rival generals and shows the prevailing mood in each of the two camps. Antony and Octavius are optimistic and united, although the shadow of disagreement passes over their camp. Their mood foreshadows victory. Brutus and Cassius are also united but pessimistic; they still disagree both in their military and philosophic decisions, but they exchange farewells in perfect harmony and friendship. The talk of omens, suicide, and philosophy foreshadows the death of Cassius and Brutus by suicide.

ACT V: SCENE II

On the battlefield at Philippi, Brutus and Messala exchange hasty words. Brutus orders Messala to ride to the legions on the other (right) side of the field to deliver written orders to Cassius. He is to make an immediate attack on Antony's wing. Then Brutus observes that Octavius' wing shows signs of weakening and orders a sudden attack to overthrow it completely.

Comment and Summary

Since it is impossible to depict a fullscale battle onstage, playwrights in various eras have used a variety of devices to convey the idea of battle without actually showing it. In ancient dramas, battles took place offstage, and messengers relayed information concerning the outcome of the battle. Shakespeare uses this classical method of establishing the atmosphere of battle without actually showing it, but he combines it with several other devices: short scenes, shifting from place to place on the field of battle to produce the effect of confusion and rapid action; some hand-to-hand combat enacted onstage; and verbal dueling, as among the generals in the preceding scene. The entire battle of Philippi is presented from the conspirators' point of view. In this scene, only Brutus and Messala are seen, but Brutus' orders describe what is taking place elsewhere on the field.

ACT V: SCENE III

Cassius and Titinius appear on another part of the field of Philippi. Cassius, seeing his men deserting, tells Titinius how he slew his ensign who was turning to run. Titinius cries that Brutus gave the word to attack Antony too early. Meanwhile, Brutus' men, having overcome Octavius, were busy plundering the enemy's camp instead of assisting Cassius' flank, which was surrounded by Antony's soldiers. Pindarus enters to warn Cassius to flee, for Antony and his men have reached his tents. Cassius answers that he has retreated far enough. Looking across the plain, he asks, "Are those my tents where I perceive the fire?" Titinius replies, "They are, my lord."

Comment

The attack ordered by Brutus has been a failure for Cassius, who has slain his own flag-bearer for deserting the field. Now Cassius rests on a hill at one end of the Philippian plain. He shows his courage and resignation by refusing to retreat farther even though the enemy is in close pursuit.

Cassius sees a body of horsemen in the distance and asks Titinius to ride to them and learn whether they are friends or foes. As Titinius rides off, Cassius orders Pindarus to climb higher on the hill to watch what is happening to Titinius, for his own "sight was ever thick" (near-sighted). As Pindarus climbs the hill, Cassius expresses his complete resignation to death: "This day I breathed first; time is come round,/ And where I did begin, there shall I end;/ My life is run his compass." Pindarus yells back to Cassius that Titinius has been surrounded by horsemen and exclaims, "He's ta'en! And hark! They shout for joy." Cassius bids Pindarus to come down, grieving that he is a coward to live so long and to see his "best friend" captured before his face. When Pindarus returns, Cassius reminds him how he had spared his life in Parthia when he had taken him captive on the condition that Pindarus swore to do whatsoever Cassius demanded. Cassius declares Pindarus a free man and orders him to take his sword, the same which ran Caesar through, and strike him in the bosom. As Pindarus guides the sword into his heart, Cassius cries, "Caesar, thou art reveng'd Even with the sword that kill'd thee." And with these words, Cassius dies. Pindarus sighs, "So I am free; yet would not so have been,/ Durst I have done my will. O Cassius!/ Far from this country Pindarus shall run,/ Where never Roman shall take note of him."

Comment

Cassius has already resigned himself to death before he is misinformed that Titinius has been captured. Ironically, he has set Pindarus to watch because his own sight is short. Equally ironic is his grief over having lived to see his best friend captured "before my face," when, in fact, he has not seen a thing. It is Cassius' pessimistic resignation and his short-sightedness which moves him to commit suicide before he has confirmed Pindarus' report. The emphasis on the fact that Cassius dies with the same sword that pierced Caesar expresses the **theme** of retribution and is an example of poetic justice, in which an ironic ending, suitable to the crime committed, is provided for the wrongdoer. Still another **irony** is suggested by Cassius' suicide, which shows his complete and misguided rejection of Epicureanism, a philosophy which held that the senses were often deceptive and created illusions which, if they produced pain, were to be rejected. Cassius as an Epicurean would have been forced to reject the false report of Titinius' capture, at least until it had been confirmed absolutely. In his final words, Cassius addresses Caesar, leaving the impression that the spirit of Caesar hovers over the field of death and has participated in his own vengeance.

Pindarus' final words before parting adds a touch of bitter humor to the somber scene by suggesting that the civilized Romans are far more barbaric than the semi-civilized Parthians.

As Pindarus leaves the Roman world for good, Titinius returns with Messala. Messala tells Titinius that they have exchanged Brutus' victory over Octavius for Antony's victory over Cassius, leaving the situation the same as at the start of the day. Titinius remarks that these tidings will comfort Cassius. Messala asks where Cassius is and learns that he is on that same hill, just as he discovers a body on the ground. When Titinius sees that it is Cassius', he cries, "Cassius is no more. O setting sun!/ As in thy red rays thou dost sink to night,/ So in his red blood Cassius' day is set;/ The sun of Rome is set. Our day is gone;/ Clouds, dews, and dangers come; our deeds are done./ Mistrust of my success hath done this deed." Messala, however, blames Cassius' suicide on his lack of confidence in their victory for Rome and on the imaginary fears produced by Cassius' melancholy and despondent nature. Titinius then asks where Pindarus is. Messala tells him to look for Pindarus, while he returns to tell Brutus the bad news.

When Messala leaves, Titinius addresses the body of his noble lord Cassius, mourning, "Alas, thou has misconstrued everything." He takes the victory garland which Brutus had given him for Cassius and places it as a sign of honor on the head of the corpse. Then, asking leave of the gods (for ending his time before their appointed hour), he expresses his duty as a Roman, picks up Cassius' sword, and kills himself.

Comment

Titinius has taken personal blame for the death of Cassius, who upon learning that Titinius his "best friend" had been captured, ended his own life. Following Cassius' example, Titinius takes the death of his friend as a sign that all is lost for their cause. He shows the loyalty and personal devotion of a true friend and proclaims it his duty as a Roman to die with Cassius. The **theme** of friendship even unto death is not a major one in this play, but it crops up from time to time as a sign of the great interest the Renaissance audience had in the concept of friendship among the ancients.

Messala returns bringing Brutus, young Cato, Strato, Volumnius, and Lucilius. Brutus asks where Cassius' body lies, and Messala points to where Titinius kneels in mourning. Brutus discovers that Titinius is dead and cries, "O Julius Caesar, thou art mighty yet!/ Thy spirit walks abroad, and turns our swords/ In our own proper entrails."

Comment

The **theme** of vengeance for Caesar's murder, echoed in Cassius' dying words, is expressed again in Brutus' cry. The battle and destruction which Antony had prophesied at Caesar's death, has, indeed, come to pass, and the spirit of Caesar has relentlessly tracked the murderers "and turns our swords/ In our own proper entrails." Brutus' own death by suicide is now ominously predicted in his last remark.

In a final tribute to his dead friends, Brutus exclaims, "Are yet two Romans living such as these?/ The last of all the Romans, fare thee well!" Brutus then orders that Cassius' body be sent to Thasos for the funeral, lest his funeral at Philippi destroy the morale of the soldiers. He bids young Cato, Lucilius, Labeo, and Flavius prepare for another battle before the night, since it is only three o'clock.

SUMMARY

The importance of this scene is the death of Cassius as the result of his own nature and his ironic misunderstanding of events. Cassius' last hours are courageous and noble ones. He has rescued his battle flag, killed a coward refused to retreat, and grieved over a captured friend. He dies not as a coward or base murderer but as a noble if misguided man, the victim of an avenging spirit, his own melancholy fears, and his own tragic flaws. The work begun on the ides of March is nearing its end. The man who devises the conspiracy against Caesar is dead. The monster of "domestic fury and fierce civil strife which Antony had set loose (III. i) is writhing to its end. Brutus and Labeo (who, according to Plutarch, had also stabbed Caesar) are the only conspirators left alive.

We can expect to see the end of them in the remaining two scenes of the play.

ACT V: SCENE IV

Brutus, Cato, Lucilius, Messala, and Flavius are seen on another part of the battlefield of Philippi. In the midst of battle, Brutus passes quickly across the stage, encouraging his men to fight bravely.

As Brutus goes off, young Cato stoutly proclaims he is the son of Marcus Cato, "a foe to tyrants, and my country's friend."

Enemy soldiers appear and engage Cato and Lucilius in single combat.

Echoing young Cato's cries, Lucilius shouts, "And I am Brutus, Marcus Brutus, I." The fighting continues. Lucilius sees young Cato fall. As he continues to fight, Lucilius pays tribute to his comrade, "O young and noble Cato, art thou down?/ Why now thou diest as bravely as Titinius."

Commanded to yield, Lucilius ceases to do battle and offers his captors gold to kill him instantly and to be honored by having slain Brutus in battle. The soldier declines the bribe, for it is a far greater honor to take the noble Brutus prisoner.

Antony arrives at this point and is told that Brutus is captured. Addressing Lucilius, Antony asks where Brutus is. Loyally, Lucilius answers, "Brutus is safe enough," He adds, "When you do find him, alive or dead,/ He will be found like Brutus, like himself" (that is, as noble as ever).

Antony informs his men that Lucilius, although he is not Brutus, is a worthy prize. He orders them to take Lucilius prisoner and to treat him kindly, for Antony would like to have him as a friend. Then others are ordered to pursue Brutus and to report to Antony at Octavius' tent.

Comment and Summary

The second engagement in the battle of Philippi is portrayed with a good deal of physical movement. Brutus rushes across the stage. There is hand-to-hand combat. Cato falls. Lucilius is captured. Lucilius follows a practice to medieval warfare in proclaiming he is Brutus. He does not wish to assume honors that are not rightfully his, but attempts to protect his generals by confusing the enemy and preventing their pursuit of the real target, Brutus. In some editions of the play, this speech is attributed to Brutus, in which case, Brutus makes an exit just before Cato falls. Plutarch makes it clear that Lucilius does impersonate Brutus.

Brief as it is, the scene shows that Brutus' men are loyal, fight courageously to the end, and are still devoted to the cause of the Republic. It shows that Brutus is slowly being defeated. His brother-in-law, young Cato, is killed; his lieutenant, Lucilius, is captured; and he himself is in flight with the enemy in hot pursuit. Antony appears briefly as shrewdly politic as ever and attempts to sabotage the rival army by expressing his desire to have Lucilius for a friend.

ACT V: SCENE V

Brutus, Dardanius, Clitus, Strato, and Volumnius appear in another part of the field. Brutus and the remnants of his army rest on a rock. Clitus reports that Statilius has sent a signal, but since he did not come back he has evidently been captured or slain. Pessimistically, Brutus replies, "Slaying is the word;/ It is a deed in fashion." Leaning closer, Brutus whispers into Clitus' ear, and Clitus responds to the message, "What, I, my lord? No, not for all the world!" Brutus then turns to Dardanius, who replies, "Shall I do such a deed?"

Clitus and Dardanius compare notes and reveal that Brutus has requested each of them to kill him. They watch him as he meditates quietly apart. "Now is that noble vessel full of grief,/ That it runs over even at his eyes," Clitus observes.

Brutus calls Volumnius to him and tells him about the ghost of Caesar, which has appeared to him twice, once at Sardis and again last night at Philippi. "I know my hour is come," Brutus declares. Volumnius tries to argue Brutus out of his depression, but Brutus is convinced that the enemy has beaten them to the pit like wild beasts. It is better, he decides, "to leap in ourselves/ Than tarry till they push us."

An alarm is sounded and Clitus warns Brutus to fly. Brutus bids his men farewell, declaring, "My heart doth joy that yet in all my life/ I found no man but he was true to me." Now he is tired and his bones crave rest. The alarm is sounded again, and warnings to fly are shouted from within. Brutus sends the others off, promising to follow. Only? Strato is asked to remain.

Brutus confronts his servant Strato with the same request he had made of his friends, and Strato agrees to hold the sword and hide his face, while Brutus ends his life.

Servant and master take hands and say goodbye. Then, with the words "Caesar, now be still;/ I killed not thee with half so good a will," Brutus runs upon his sword and dies.

A retreat is sounded as Brutus dies. Antony and Octavius arrive on the scene. They have with them Messala and Lucilius who have been taken prisoner. Octavius speaks first, "What man is that," he asks, pointing to Strato. Messala identifies Brutus' servant and asks Strato where Brutus is. "Free from the bondage you are in, Messala," Strato replies. Brutus has killed himself, "and no man else hath honor in his death." Lucilius praises Brutus' suicide, which proves to him that Brutus was as honorable as he had thought.

Octavius offers to take Brutus' men into his service, and Strato agrees to go if Messala gives him a recommendation. Learning that Strato held the sword for Brutus, Messala urges Octavius to take this good servant as his follower.

Antony, who has been silent all the while, speaks now over the body of Brutus: "This was the noblest Roman of them all./ All the conspirators save only he/ Did that they did in envy of great Caesar;/ He, only in a general honest thought/ And common good to all, made one of them." Antony concludes his eulogy of Brutus by describing his nature as gentle "and the elements/ So mixed in him that Nature might stand up/ And say to all the world, 'This was a man!'"

It is Octavius who has the last words in the play. He orders that Brutus be given "all respect and rites of burial" and that within Octavius' tent "his bones tonight shall lie,/ Most like a soldier, ordered honorably."

Comment and Summary

The last **climax** of the play is reached with Brutus' death. His presumptuousness and arrogant virtue disintegrated in death, Brutus has honor and dignity restored to him in his last hours. He has fought courageously and has faced death with the resignation becoming a great man. In the last scene, he is seen as the object of devotion of his surviving friends, who refuse to hold the sword on which he dies. He is rid of his obstinate constancy to impracticable ideals and acts by human impulse when he decides on suicide. Lucilius, Messala, and Strato applaud his honorable death, and Octavius promises funeral rites in which Brutus' honor as a soldier will be recognized. Antony sums up the character of Brutus as it has been seen throughout the play. Brutus was "the noblest Roman of them all," the only one of the conspirators who killed Caesar out of a concern for the public good and not for envy or in the hope of personal gain.

The avenging spirit of Caesar is never seen again, except as Brutus reports it as an omen of his defeat. Clearly, it is Brutus' belief as he dies that the work begun on the ides of March has been finished, the pleasure of the Fates has been decided, and the spirit of Caesar has been avenged.

The final **episode** of the play is like a prologue to another. It shows Octavius emerging as the most dominant member of the triumvirate. He speaks first and last and gives all the commands for the disposition of Brutus' men and his body. Then, for the first time in the entire play, Antony praises Brutus. There is a touch of pathos in the fact that his eulogy of the man he had pursued to his death had its counterpart in previous and subsequent events. Brutus has so praised Causer, the man he had slain;

now Antony praises the man he has hunted to the pit; and later, Octavius praises Antony after he has haunted him to his death. This eulogy over his victim suggests that Antony will take over Brutus' role as the man marked for extinction by the gods, just as Brutus had taken over Caesar's, and the clash between Antony and Octavius, which is dramatized in Shakespeare's *Antony and Cleopatra*, is foreshadowed in this closing scene of *Julius Caesar.*

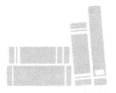

JULIUS CAESAR

. . . .

Julius Caesar

In Shakespeare's play, not the Caesar of the Gallic wars, described in Plutarch's *Life of Caesar* and reflected in Caesar's own *Commentaries.* He is the aging Caesar, physically infirm, but successful and overconfident, who, according to Plutarch, had overreached himself, insulted his peers, and incurred the wrath of patricians, Republicans, and the gods. According to the dramatic chronology and Cassius' reports, Caesar has recently suffered from fever in Spain and is now deaf and epileptic. At the opening of the play, apart from his costume and the pomp and circumstance which accompany his appearance, Caesar displays few of the special virtues which had made him a conqueror and dictator and favorite of the common people. Of late, he has begun to stand on ceremony (religious ritual and superstition), which is a sign of his mental deterioration. He is concerned with sacrifice and augury, with prodigies, and with Calpurnia's dream. He is subject to flattery and is vain and boastful. But to call him a coward is to do him an injustice. He agrees to stay home from the Senate out of consideration for Calpurnia's fears, but when he is told the decision would be misconstrued, or ridiculed, or that he might never be offered the crown again, he alters his decision. His human tenderness is subordinated to his public image and his ambition.

Despite his shortcomings, some of the heroic traits and gracious attributes which belonged to the historical Caesar come through in Shakespeare's characterization. His insight into Cassius shows he is still a shrewd judge of men, and his public bequests betoken his political wisdom even after his death. His friends attest to his military powers, his justice, and his generosity; Brutus, his murderer, finds no fault in his past actions; and even Cassius, his worst enemy, admits that Caesar never abused him as Brutus has. Caesar is almost tender in his dealings with Calpurnia and Decius; he is paternal to Antony when he instructs and praises him, and he is urbane and hospitable to the conspirators when they call at his home.

In the Senate, on the day of his death, Caesar reaches the height of his ruthlessness and self-assurance, which had once made him a hero. He has forgotten his human limitations in his rise to power. He tempts the gods when he declares himself above "ordinary men," comparing his own constancy with that of the North Star, and he enrages his friends when he obstinately refuses their petitions, although they implore him on their knees to grant mercy to a banished Roman.

After he is stricken, his humanity is restored to him. The dying Caesar is not the infatuated man who has just spoken from the throne. For a moment, he is an Elizabethan idealist who cherishes the noble love of a friend more than anything in the world. When he sees Brutus, whom he loves best, among his betrayers, he relinquishes his hold on the world: "Then fall Caesar."

Brutus

He is first seen in the play as the bemused observer of Caesar's procession as Caesar marches to the Lupercalia. He is not a "gamesome" fellow and does not choose to join the festivities. Of late, he has shown ungentle looks and has made Caesar fear he has lost his love. Upon hearing shouts from the market-place where Caesar is presiding, Brutus inadvertently expresses his fear that Caesar has become king. From that moment on, he is forced to end his contemplations and make a decision for action.

His conflict consists of his love for Caesar on one hand, and his concern for the public good and the welfare of the Republic on the other. Persuaded by Cassius to join a conspiracy against Caesar, Brutus spends a restless night making his decision. He can find no justification for Caesar's murder in Caesar's past actions; therefore, he finds justification for it in what Caesar might become. He assumes that Caesar will become an unbearable tyrant if he is made king, and on the basis of this assumption he decides to murder him. The flaw in his reasoning is that Brutus does not raise the question of whether or not a moral end justifies immoral means, nor does he consider that his action may be met with public disfavor. He is blindly convinced in the power of reason and believes that the public, when they have heard his reasons, will support his action.

Because he has little practical knowledge of life, he is blind to the real motives and characters of men and is ignorant of the practical means of conducting a war. He trusts Antony who betrays him, rejects Cicero who is as loyal to the same Republican cause as he, and mistrusts Cassius who loves him. He refuses to obtain money by unjust means at Sardis, yet becomes indignant because Cassius has not sent him some of the tainted money that Cassius has obtained. He even falsely accuses Cassius of personal corruption.

He is seen at the height of his arrogance and self-confidence, obstinate idealism, and incorruptibility when, like Caesar, he is being least merciful, least human, least yielding to his friend, Cassius. Despite his show of confidence during this quarrel with Cassius, Brutus spends a restless night in his tent. Disturbed over the reaction of the mob to the murder of Caesar, empassioned by the argument he has had with Cassius, and grieving over the death of his noble wife, Portia, Brutus sees an apparition. The ghost, which is either a subjective projection of Brutus' disturbed mind, or the existing spirit of the unavenged Caesar, tells Brutus that he is his "evil spirit" and will see him again at Philippi.

Courageously, Brutus decides to meet his destiny at once. He is no longer in torment when he sets out for Philippi, for the resolution of his conflict is in sight. Either he will be victor of the day or he will be killed in battle, and the work begun on the ides of March will have been done. It is this impatience to see the end which causes Brutus to act impetuously, bringing about destruction to Cassius, to the cause of the Republic, and finally to himself.

His death by suicide is in opposition to the philosophic principles he has professed all his life, and which he claimed he would continue to follow even if defeated. This suicide is the one compromise with his ideals that Brutus is known to make in the play, for it is an act which he had previously regarded as "cowardly and vile." Yet this act wins him continued honor among his friends and the praise of his enemy, Antony, for the first time in the play.

Cassius

An able soldier and a shrewd politician. He is the real organizer of the conspiracy against Caesar, which he enters out of his love of freedom as much as out of his hatred for Caesar and tyranny. When he is first seen in the play, he expresses his fear that he has lost the friendship and approval of Brutus, whom he loves and respects. Assured of Brutus' continuing love for him, Cassius tries to persuade his friend to join the anti-Caesarist cause. Cassius' imprecations against Caesar show a certain blindness to the spirit of leadership, which Caesar still has, and an overemphasis on physical strength, which Caesar no longer possesses.

Seen next from Caesar's point of view, Cassius "has a lean and hungry look;/ He thinks too much." He is a man to be feared because "he reads much,/ He is a great observer, and he looks/ Quite through the deeds of men. He loves no plays,/ ... he hears no music;/ Seldom he smiles, and smiles in such a sort/ As if he mocked himself and scorned his spirit/ That could be moved to smile at anything./ Such men as he be never at heart's ease/ Whiles they behold a greater than themselves,/ And therefore are they very dangerous." Caesar's description is that of a melancholy man, who is also a cynic (in our sense of the word). Cassius is a silent type, observant, penetrating, quick to anger, slow to smile. He abjures the sensual pleasures of life such as Antony enjoys, but he is well-read and thoughtful. He knows the philosophy of Stoicism, but claims he could never live by its ideals, and he knows that he cannot accept Portia's death with stoic resignation as Brutus does. He is by admission (and historically) an Epicurean, who believes in friendship as one of the highest forms of good and disbelieves in the divine intervention in human affairs. His interpretation of the amazing prodigies on the eve of the ides of March must be regarded as a ruse to attract

Casca to the conspiracy, for surely, as an Epicurean, he cannot believe in omens. On the other hand, Cassius announces late in the play that he has discarded Epicureanism and now accepts omens as warnings from the gods to men. Perhaps the conversion is supposed to have taken place prior to the events of the play. (Although Shakespeare does not provide this information, Cassius' philosophic conversion is said to have taken place just before the assassination of Caesar (see Plutarch). If this is true in the play as well, then, as the play progresses, Cassius' character changes philosophically as well as psychologically.)

Early in the play, Cassius' plan to persuade Brutus to join his cause makes him seem like a Machiavellian villain who seduces the noble Brutus in order to use him as a puppet; thus, Brutus appears to be exalted by this contrast with the conniving Cassius, and when he wins decisions over Cassius, his victories seem to be just. Shakespeare makes it clear, however, that Brutus' decisions are based on impractical ideals and Cassius' suggestions, although ignoble, are workable ones. As the play progresses, Brutus' character deteriorates; he becomes overconfident, obstinate, cruel, and taunting. Cassius, meanwhile, begins to display the "rash choler" of his melancholy nature. At the same time, he reveals that the love, a respect, and honor he shows for Brutus are unquestionably real. Cassius ultimately submits to chastisement for practicing certain military expediencies which Brutus regards as corrupt, and acknowledges his subordination to Brutus by calling him "my lord." His submission is so complete that he follows Brutus to Philippi against his better judgment, changes his philosophy to Stoicism in order to meet his destiny with greater resignation, and ends his life in a burst of melancholic depression in which imaginary fears and delusions of imminent defeat overcome him entirely. Already depressed over the ill-timed venture at Philippi, Cassius seizes upon the supposed capture of his "best friend" Titinius as a final reason for ending his life. His trusted slave Pindarus "guides" the sword, which had killed Caesar, and Cassius dies, guiltily crying, "Caesar thou art revenged."

Mark Antony

One of the foremost opportunists of his day. Historically, he was interested in only one thing, political power. In the play, however, Antony is portrayed as a well-rounded Roman or a perfect Elizabethan gentleman. He is an athlete, likes music, and enjoys plays. He is given to all-night carousing, but does not shirk his duties by sleeping late. He is loyal and devoted to Caesar, almost subservient to the man he loves, honors, and fears. He is misjudged by Brutus as a harmless fellow and a mere lover of pleasure, but he is seen as shrewd and dangerous by the more perceptive Cassius. Antony wisely pretends to throw in his lot with the conspirators in order to gain time and favors, but as soon as he can, he plans to let loose an unholy reign of terror to avenge the death of his beloved lord. The mischief he sets afoot is so clever and cruel that he becomes a Machiavellian figure for a time. His gifts of oratory, his political acumen, and his knowledge of mob psychology have been hidden from men, but they are all disclosed during his famous funeral oration, delivered in verse over the body of Caesar. It is seen during the oration that Antony's indulgence in the company of men and in the arts, especially poetry and drama, have served as an education in political leadership.

Antony is next seen ruthlessly signing death warrants of political enemies-seventy or one hundred, according to the reports, including Cicero and his own nephew. He displays Machiavellian statesmanship in these political murders and in his plan to get rid of Lepidus when he has finished using him. His ambition and greed come forward when he flinches at sharing a third of the world with a mulish dullard like Lepidus.

At the end of the play, Antony shows his skill in verbal and physical combat. He is confidently, even smugly, assured of victory over the conspirators, and he still speaks of avenging Caesar, despite his previously expressed interest in gaining control over Rome. Octavius begins to show his teeth, however, and in the final scene of the play, takes full command over the business at hand. Antony is silent in Octavius' presence, but he delivers a final eulogy over the body of Brutus in which he praises his enemy for the first time in the play, suggesting that since Octavius has taken over, Antony has had some cause to sympathize with Brutus' fight against tyranny.

Octavius

The grand-nephew of Caesar, was adopted as Caesar's son and heir, inheriting Caesar's name, three-fourths of his estate, and Caesar's lust for power and control over Rome. Octavius first appears in the play after Caesar's death. He joins the triumvirate formed by Antony and Lepidus and follows the plans and directions of Antony, even agreeing to eliminate Lepidus. Privately, however, he feels that Lepidus is a tried and valiant man, who deserves to be rewarded for good service. At his second appearance at the battle of Philippi, Octavius is beginning to balk at Antony's command, accepts orders this time, but threatens to cross Antony at a later date. By the end of the battle and the play, Octavius is in full command. He does most of the talking, gets no opposition from Antony, gives orders for Brutus' funeral, recruits men from Brutus' ranks, and calls the field to rest, all in the presence of Antony, who remains silent except for a final, pathetic eulogy over the body of Brutus.

Portia

A heroic example of the devoted Roman wife. She has a noble husband, Brutus, and a noble father, Cato, whose courage and wisdom she feels she has inherited. Concerned for her husband, she explains in great detail the reasons for her anxiety and implores him to tell her the cause of her grief. She is not put off by pretexts and uses reason and flattery to get to the truth, which she claims it is her right to know.

As she says, she is more than an ordinary woman, for she is Brutus' wife and Cato's daughter, and has proved her constancy and resolution by spilling her own blood when she thought it necessary. Although she wins the argument and learns of Brutus' plans, she has great difficulty the next day in keeping herself from divulging the plans inadvertently. She admits that it is hard for women to keep counsel, but manages to do so. She becomes a study in anxiety as she awaits news of the outcome of the assassination. Later, her anxiety over Brutus' absence causes her to commit suicide. Her death is received with stoic resignation by Brutus.

Because of her spirited and intelligent argument, her occasional use of legal terminology, and her delicate sexual conversation, Portia's characterization is sometimes taken as a prototype of the later Portia, heroine of *The Merchant of Venice*.

Calpurnia

The superstitious and barren wife of Julius Caesar, whom she loves and obeys. Her fears of omens is recently acquired, for she "never stood on ceremonies" in her earlier days. Now, however, strange dreams, ominous prodigies, and fateful augurs have frightened her. She fears for her husband's life and implores him to stay at home and guard his safety on the ides of March. She thinks of Caesar as a prince and believes that the falling meteors are warnings of a prince's death. When she hears her husband boast that he is more dangerous than danger itself, she recognizes that this is foolish arrogance and tells him so; "Alas, my lord/ Your wisdom is consumed in confidence." In response to her criticism and humble petitions, Caesar momentarily agrees to satisfy her whim. However, she is last seen accepting chastisement silently ("How foolish do your fears seem now") and obediently fetching Caesar's robe as he flouts her wishes and leaves for the Senate.

Decius Brutus

A member of the conspiracy against Caesar. His real name was Decimus Brutus, but Shakespeare followed North's translation of Plutarch where Decius had appeared. Decius volunteers to assure Caesar's arrival at the Senate on the ides of March. He is aware of Caesar's assumed disgust for flattery and plans to flatter Caesar by praising this disgust. He uses his friendship with Caesar and Caesar's love for him to elicit Caesar's excuse for absenting himself from the Senate. Then he cleverly reinterprets Calpurnia's dreams which prevents Caesar from going out, and shrewdly converts it to an auspicious one. Decius manipulates Caesar through the latter's fear of ridicule, his ambition for the crown, and his fear of insulting the Senate. When he finally gets Caesar on his way, Decius contrives to keep him from reading Artemidorus' warning by interposing another letter, purportedly from Trebonius. Thus, he prevents Caesar from reading one letter by giving him a second, and seems to know that Caesar will be easily confused and decide to read none. After the assassination, he disappears from the play, but it is presumed here, as it occurred in history, that Antony has Decius murdered.

Casca

An amusing and informative conspirator. He first appears as a member of Caesar's train who has attended the Lupercal and observed the attempted coronation and Caesar's reactions to it. He describes these events to Cassius and Brutus in a ludicrous satirical style with more than a hint of rudeness and vulgarity. The whole coronation **episode**, to Casca's thinking, is "mere foolery," a phrase he repeats more than once during his description. Brutus views him as a "blunt fellow" who used to have a " quick mettle" when they went to school together, but Cassius explains that Casca still has a lively disposition when it is needed for some bold or noble enterprise. (It is Casca, in fact, who strikes the first blow at Caesar.) According to Cassius, Casca's rudeness and sluggish appearance are donned to disguise his good intelligence so that when he speaks the truth, men will be slow to take offense at an apparent fool.

Not long after this, however, Casca is seen as a trembling clown, amazed, confused, and frightened by the wonders of the night and unable to make sense out of the portents. He fears that the gods are angry and that the end of the world had come. Cassius easily persuades Casca, whom he calls "dull," that the impatience of heaven is a warning of the abnormal state of affairs in Rome, and that an ordinary man like Caesar has become a fearful monster.

Fear and Casca are often found together. Casca believes "it is the part of men to fear and tremble," and he regards one who dies early as one who "cuts off so many years of fearing death." Casca is associated with cowardice when Cassius tells him that he lacks courage ("those sparks of life That should be in a Roman,") or else that he does not use it, and again when Antony sarcastically calls him "my valiant Casca" and when Antony claims that Casca stabbed Caesar in the back. Although Casca signals the attack against Caesar and strikes the first blow, it may be inferred that Casca's participation in the "bold or noble enterprise" of Caesar's assassination is the act of a coward. (Shakespeare does not reveal Casca's fate after the assassination, but history records that he killed himself after the battle of Philippi.)

Other Conspirators

Trebonius who lures Antony away from the Senate while Caesar is being murdered; Metellus Cimber who had a personal grudge against Caesar for exiling his brother, Publius Cimber; Cinna, a messenger for the conspirators, who had the same name as Cinna the poet; Ligarius who gets out of a sickbed to join the conspiracy.

Cicero

He has a minor role in the play and is used mainly to create the atmosphere of the period in which the play takes place. Cicero was well known to Elizabethans as a famous orator and an ardent Republican; his absence from the conspiracy is given some explanation in the play.

Lepidus

The third and weakest member of the triumvirate, consisting also of Antony and Octavius. He appears only briefly, and is rather a subject of discussion between Antony and Octavius than a character in the play.

Members Of Brutus' Army And Household

Lucilius, a trusted and loyal lieutenant; Lucius, a devoted young slave and flute player; Strato, the slave who assists in Brutus' death; Volumnius, Cato the Younger, Varro, Clitus, Claudius, Dardanius, and Messala, a loyal follower who joins Antony after Brutus' death.

Members Of Cassius' Troop And Household

Titinius, Cassius "best friend,' whose capture is the immediate cause of Cassius' suicide; Pindarus, the Parthian slave of Cassius, who assists in his death.

Other Minor Characters

Publius, the venerable Roman senator, who is terrified by the assassination and says not a word in the play; Flavius and Marullus, tribunes of the people, followers of Pompey, and defenders of the Republic, who chastise the mob for celebrating Caesar's triumph; Cinna the Poet, a friend of Caesar's who is torn apart by the mob for having the same name as Cinna the conspirator; Artemidorus, a teacher of rhetoric, who tries to warn Caesar; the Soothsayer, who also tries to warn Caesar of the conspiracy; Popilius Lena, the senator who wishes Cassius good luck on his venture and then walks off to speak to Caesar, terrifying the assassins with possible betrayal; a cynical poet, who attempt to reconcile Cassius and Brutus after their quarrel.

The Mob

The mob has an important role in many of Shakespeare's plays, especially *Coriolanus,* but is nowhere more significant than in *Julius Caesar*. Here they are seen as an Elizabethan rather than as a Roman mob. They are a capricious lot who love holidays and pageants. They turn out early, climb high towers with babes in arms, and sit all day waiting for a procession to go by. They hiss what offends them and cheer what they like. They have a mass will and a mass mind which can easily be persuaded and easily enraged. Once it is enraged, it is impossible to reason with the mob. Then they are quick to take insult and merciless in their punishment of slight offenses. No individual in the mob would kill a man because of his name, but as a mob, they kill for a name or for no reason at all. They have "chopt hands" and "sweaty night-caps," and utter such a deal of stinking breath (onions were staples in the diet of lower-class Elizabethans) because Caesar refused the crown, that it almost choked Caesar; "for he swounded and fell down at it."

JULIUS CAESAR

CRITICAL COMMENTARY

. . . .

INTRODUCTION

Julius Caesar is one of Shakespeare's most popular and enduring plays. It has been so for nearly four hundred years and has withstood the changes of time and taste. Different ages had different reasons for enjoying the tragedy, but for each, the play had some special appeal. For Elizabethans, that special appeal was the resemblance between Caesar and some of their more tragic kings. For our own age, the political, ethical, and psychological implications are of primary interest.

The play was almost certainly produced originally in 1599 at the Globe theater. Contemporary **allusions** to it, and the frequency of its production, make it clear that it had a profound effect on its early audiences. During the seventeenth century, it was performed at the courts of James I, Charles I, and, later, Charles II. It was one of the few plays which was not revised to meet the so-called classical standards of the Restoration era, although critics of both the Restoration and Augustan eras of English literature had difficulty in reconciling *Julius Caesar* with the Aristotelian unities and rules of decorum. Romantic critics of the nineteenth century turned their attention on the characters of the play, and in the liberal spirit of the age tended to favor Brutus as the hero of the play over Caesar the tyrant and villain of the piece.

In our own time, critics have taken many new approaches in attempting to answer fundamental problems, raised in the play, which have vexed thinkers since the play was first produced. The structural unity of the play, the identity of the hero, the real **theme** of the play, and the author's moral attitude toward insurrection, have all been open to question. Its **genre**, too, has been questioned, and has been identified by some modern critics as a "problem play" in which the central interest is a moral-political psychological problem rather than a tragic hero.

THE STRUCTURE OF THE PLAY

If *Julius Caesar* was produced in 1599, it was performed not long after Shakespeare's chronicle play *Henry V* had been seen on the boards. It is easy to see the chronicle's influence on the loose construction and episodic treatment which the Roman tragedy received. Because of its loose composition, critics have argued that there are two parts to the play and two heroes, Brutus and Caesar. Others like George Lyman Kittredge have insisted on the structural unity of the play, pointing out that Caesar's spirit takes over after Caesar's death and remains in the background for the remainder of the play.

The historian and literary critic Louis B. Wright, who has probed deeply into the character of the Elizabethan audience, agrees with Kittdredge that Caesar is the central interest and provides the unity of the play: "To Elizabethans, Caesar was a character of consuming interest. They were vastly interested in strong men who could impose order in a chaotic world.... Caesar had been a leader with the capacity for rule such as Elizabethans understood and approved."

The Victorian critic R. G. Moulton produced an elaborate analysis of the structure of the play as the movement of Passion. In doing so, however, he could not avoid the inevitable issue of the hero of the play. Moulton chose Caesar as the hero, for he believed that the **climax** of the play occurs in the center rather than at the end. Such an early **climax**, Moulton declared, might create a tediously long conclusion in the work of other writers, but Shakespeare's dramatic genius prevents this loss of interest in the remainder of the play by making Antony appear immediately after the murder as the avenger of his dead lord. There is a transitional stage in which the play lags somewhat after Antony's oration, but new interest arises when Cassius and Brutus quarrel and become reconciled. In this master stroke of human characterization, Moulton declared, Shakespeare revives audience interest in the decline of the two chief conspirators and prevents a lag of interest in the waning action of the play.

Ever since the eighteenth century, critics have felt that Brutus, not Caesar, was the central interest in the play and provided its structural unity from beginning to end. Voltaire was among the first of many who believed that *Julius Caesar* was a misnomer and that the tragedy should rightly be called Marcus Brutus. Sir Mungo William MacCallum (1910), supported by Dover Wilson, also saw Brutus as the character who determined the unity of the play. MacCallum argued that *Julius Caesar* was a transitional play between Shakespeare's histories and his tragedies and pointed out that in a number of Shakespeare's historical plays, the titular hero dies before the end of the play. In 2 *Henry IV*, for example, the play continues for an entire act after King Henry's death, while in all of Shakespeare's tragedies, the hero remains in focus until the end of the play.

When modern critics approach the problem of the structure of *Julius Caesar*, they often base their analyses on the assumption that the hero of the play is deliberately made ambiguous and that the **theme** of rebellion or insurrection is the real focus of Shakespeare's interest. Under these circumstances, the unity of the play is not found in a single hero, but in its ironic contrasts of characters and events and in its style and **imagery**. Brents Stirling (1951), for example, finds that the **theme** of religious ritual dominates the assassination scene and that Brutus' failure to make a sacrifice out of the murder is the result of Shakespeare's intention to give the theme satirical treatment. Leo Kirschbaum (1949) tried to put Brutus back into the perspective from which he was removed by Romantic critics, who had concentrated on character analyses, believing that characters were the most important interests in Shakespeare's plays. Kirschbaum argued that Shakespeare deliberately "invented the blood-bath" in order to shock us into seeing that "murder is in the act savage and inhuman" and that regardless of its purpose "the merciless rending of a man is an obscene performance."

In his study of style and **imagery** in *Julius Caesar*, R. A. Foakes (1954) discovered that the **themes** of superstition, sickness, noise, and names, which run through the play and comprise its fabric, also determine that the unity of the play is to be found in the **theme** of rebellion. There is a good deal of concurrence among moderns like Harley Granville-Barker (1947) and Leonard F. Dean (1961) that the political **theme** of the play constitutes its focus and provides its unity. (From the point of view of staging the play, however, Granville-Barker finds that Shakespeare's sympathy rests with Brutus, although he does not wish to justify Caesar's assassination.) In an essay by Ernest

Schanzer (1955), *Julius Caesar* is declared "one of Shakespeare's most perplexing plays," for Schanzer believes that Shakespeare created a deliberately ambiguous Caesar to show up the futility of assassination. In other words, the moral and political **theme** of assassination determines its unity for Schanzer and provides the frame of reference for understanding the ambiguous natures of the characters in the play.

THE CHARACTER OF CAESAR

It is inevitable that Caesar himself should be the subject of wide critical interest. As has already been seen, the attitude of the critic toward the structural unity of the play is always brought to bear on his interpretation of the characters in the play. The conservative opinion, represented by George Lyman Kittredge, is that Caesar is central to the play from start to finish. Another conservative in his approach to Caesar is James E. Phillips, Jr. (1940), who finds that "in the character which he gives Caesar as a ruler, Shakespeare makes it clear that such autocracy was a blessing to the state. Caesar is represented as ably qualified, according to Renaissance standards, to exercise 'the specialty of rule,' There are, to be sure, personality weaknesses...."

There is a very little argument about the fact that Shakespeare depicts Caesar's physical infirmities, but there is considerable debate on whether or not Shakespeare creates a general impression of Caesar's greatness at any point in the play. MacCallum argued that Shakespeare's Caesar was a heroic figure to the audience for whom he was originally intended and that it is only through minute analysis that his defects are discovered. Professor Harry Morgan Ayres (1910) supported the argument for Caesar as the central figure of the play, but showed that he was created in the Renaissance stage tradition of the Marlovian or Senecan stage tyrant, a great and ambitious man whose heroic success produced a mad arrogance which presaged his destruction. Louis B. Wright (1958), insisting on the historical approach, asserts "If Caesar on Shakespeare's stage sounds pompous to us, his manner was not objectionable to the spectator at the Globe." Nevertheless, observers like Maynard Mack (1960), who interprets Caesar's superstitions as signs of his childishness, continue to find Caesar defective, while others like Ernest Schanzer stress the ambiguity and pathos in Caesar's portrayal. The questions still remain: Is Caesar simply the heroic and ambitious figure of history; is he purely a defective creature who deserves his bloody fate; or is he the pathetic, complex, and ambiguous figure who symbolizes the **theme** of insurrection in a problem play?

THE CHARACTER OF BRUTUS

Brutus has always aroused more interest among critics than any other character in the play. As early as the eighteenth-century, Brutus was considered by some to be the central figure of the play and the character for whom the play should be named. Samuel Johnson, the great eighteenth-century editor of Shakespeare's works, who found Julius Caesar "cold and oppressing" on the whole, was moved by "the contention and reconciliation of Brutus and Cassius."Coleridge (c. 1812) was perplexed but decidedly interested in Brutus' mental processes and in his anxiety to harmonize Brutus with his "historical preconception' of him. Coleridge probed the question, "How ... could Brutus say he finds no personal cause for the murder; i.e. none in Caesar's past conduct as a man? Had he not passed the Rubicon? ..." Equally romantic and sympathetic in his approach to Brutus, William Hazlitt (1817) views the character as a demonstration of Shakespeare's "penetration into political character." The whole design of the play, according to Hazlitt, is Brutus' attempt to liberate Rome, an attempt which "fails from the generous temper and overweening confidence of Brutus in the goodness of their cause and the assistance of others. Thus it has always been. Those who mean well themselves think well of others and fall a prey to their security."

The Danish biographer and critic George M. Brandes brought events in Shakespeare's life and times to bear on his interpretation of the play and also chose Brutus as the true hero. Brandes believed that the unsuccessful conspiracy against Queen Elizabeth by Southampton and Essex, two of Shakespeare's friends, had shown Shakespeare how "proud and nobly-disposed characters might easily be seduced into political error." In addition, Brandes maintained, Shakespeare, then at the height of his career, had begun to show an interest in noble characters like Brutus and Hamlet, whose fortunes had turned against them. Moreover, Brandes asserted, Plutarch did not appreciate Caesar's greatness, and Shakespeare, who followed Plutarch so closely in other respects, adopted Plutarch's attitude toward Caesar as well. Brutus, therefore, was selected as the tragic hero of *Julius Caesar*. As a result Caesar was belittled into a "miserable creature" of a tyrant in order to supply Brutus with a reliable motive for murder. According to Brandes, Caesar is a villain for attempting "to introduce monarchy into a well-ordered republican state," and Brutus is made "simple and great" at Caesar's expense.

Like Brandes, MacCallum found justification in Plutarch for Shakespeare's exaltation of Brutus and downgrading of Caesar. He believed, as Voltaire had more than a century earlier, that the proper title of the play should have been Marcus Brutus, for he felt that Shakespeare had made Brutus the spokesman for the Republic, which the playwright favored, and Caesar the spokesman for imperialism, which Shakespeare opposed. According to MacCallum, "Shakespeare wishes to portray a patriotic gentleman of the best Roman or the best English type...." Brutus' only flaw (as Hazlitt also saw it) is his too strict adherence to the virtues he possesses. The career of Brutus, according to MacCallum, is one of disillusionment and defeat, which reaches its **climax** in the quarrel he has with Cassius. Echoing Hazlitt, MacCallum wrote, Brutus has been "impractical and perverse, as every enthusiast for abstract justice must be, who lets himself be seduced into crime on the plea of duty, and yet shapes his course as though he were not a criminal." At the end, MacCallum declares, Brutus dies a martyr.

MacCallum's extreme justification of the nobility of Brutus is received with disfavor in many quarters, even among critics like Granville-Barker (1927), who felt that Shakespeare's sympathies were with Brutus. Granville-Barker tempers his interpretation of Brutus by insisting that Shakespeare did not intend to justify Caesar's assassination when he gave Brutus sympathetic treatment. Sir Mark Hunter approaches the play as a study in character, an approach generally rejected by younger critics, but Sir Mark does not make Brutus a stereotype of virtue as MacCallum had. He finds Brutus "noble-hearted and sincere beyond question, [but] he is intellectually dishonest." He is fanatical, self-righteous, and inconsistent. Sir Mark perceives that Brutus' "own conduct, apart from the capital crime, is sometimes at strange variance with principles simultaneously professed."

More recently, however, the studies of John Palmer (1948) have led him to conclude that Shakespeare has made Brutus the object of ironic **satire**. Cassius is the foil who first brings out Brutus' deficiencies; later Antony replaces Cassius in this function. Brutus, according to Palmer, is the portrait of an ineffectual politician whose confused thinking is "sharply divorced from political reality." But Brutus has a double nature, a private personality as well as a public image. His scenes with Portia show his private tenderness and his quarrel with Cassius reveals his real disturbance over her death, while his public show of resignation to the news of her death is in the "high Roman fashion" which Brutus assumes as his public image.

In spite of John Palmer's complex handling of the dual character of Brutus, there are still critics who view Brutus as the Romantics had. However, increased knowledge of Elizabethan history and thought has now been brought to bear on these arguments, supporting the nobility of Brutus. Bernard R. Breyer (1954), for example, expresses this view: "Brutus is, according to my theory, the good tyrannicide [and], it cannot have made the audience very happy to see him fall at the hands of the tyrant's avengers...."

JULIUS CAESAR

Question: What is the relationship between Brutus and Cassius?

Answer: Brutus and Cassius are friends of long standing who, as opposite types, have apparently fallen out with each other many times. When they are first seen in conversation, Cassius expresses the fear that Brutus no longer loves him; he suggests that he is the more dependent member of the friendship when he is happy to learn that Brutus' "ungentle" eyes are not directed at him. Apparently inconsequential, this subtle exchange between the two men sets up the relationship they continue to have with each other for the remainder of the play. Cassius is an intelligent man, a keen observer of human nature; he makes practical decisions of questionable morality, but he admires and honors the virtue and reputation of his friend Brutus and is too dependent on his love to oppose his friend for very long.

Although their conflicting natures are never forgotten, there are two major scenes in which the differences between the men are brought into sharpest focus. The first is the meeting of the conspirators in Brutus' garden, where Brutus rejects without compromise three of Cassius' proposals. He refuses to kill Antony, refuses to swear an oath, and refuses to invite Cicero to join the conspiracy. In each case, Cassius' suggestions are based on sound practical reasons. In each case Brutus' rejections are based on his constancy to moral principles. In every case, Cassius submits to Brutus' decisions, not without some argument.

The second scene in which the idealistic and practical natures of the two men are contrasted is the famous Quarrel Scene, which takes place in Sardis. Here Cassius' emotional dependence on Brutus' love is most visible, and Brutus' coldly rational appraisal of his friend's behavior is given its most extreme expression. The argument concerns practical corruption vs. absolute morality in the conduct of war. Despite his conviction that a general must overlook petty corruption and sometimes use unjust means for obtaining funds, Cassius finds his own position untenable in the face of the higher morality of Brutus, whom he reveres. Brutus is immovable to his friends' frailties of judgment and nature. He provokes Cassius' choleric disposition to greater shows of rashness and cruelly taunts him with a promise to mock (reject) him, which he knows Cassius cannot endure. Cassius is brutally pushed to the point where he asks Brutus to kill him. Having reached its nadir, the argument can go no farther, and a reconciliation takes place in which Cassius makes most of the apologies. At the close of the scene, Cassius' opposition is completely enfeebled. He protests only once more to Brutus' decision to attack the enemy on level ground rather than take the defensive from the vantage point in Sardis. At the close of the scene, Cassius addresses Brutus as "my lord." His submission is so total that he never argues with Brutus again. In the final moments before battle, he asks Brutus how he plans to face defeat if it should come. When he cannot make Brutus realize that his choice may be capture or suicide, he simply bids him a fond farewell.

Thus, the relationship between Brutus and Cassius is that of friendly antagonists. Allies in the conspiracy, they differ in every other respect. Their humors, philosophies, morals, and ideals are at odds at every point. There can be little doubt that Cassius and Brutus are intended as foils for each other, through which the characters can be examined in all their complex ramifications.

Question: What is Antony's function in the play?

Answer: Although Antony appears briefly in the early part of the play as the loyal follower of Caesar, he does not emerge as an important participant until after the assassination of Caesar.

Before the assassination, careful suggestions are planted about Antony's nature, which do not take on meaning until later in the play. He is a man who enjoys plays, music, games, and the company of men, but he is unfailing in his duty and rises early to attend to affairs of state even when he has been reveling all night. He spends a go d deal of time with Caesar, and seems to be taking lessons from him on the natures of men. After the assassination, it appears that Antony has learned his lessons well. He has judged Brutus wisely as an honorable man and accepts his promise of a safe conduct in order to gain the shrewd advantage of speaking to the crowd. Left alone with the body of Caesar, Antony's soliloquy reveals that he has taken upon himself the role of Caesar's avenger. Thus, along with Caesar's ghost, Antony is to function as an agent of revenge against the group of insurgents who have assassinated the ruler of Rome.

During his funeral oration, Antony reveals that he has tremendous powers as an orator and political manipulator, which had long been hidden under his apparent role as a lover of pleasure. Like young princes in Shakespeare's history plays (especially Prince Hal in *Henry IV* Part I), Antony has feigned profligacy while he bided his time. Now he bursts forth in all his glory as the leader and manipulator of men. The funeral oration shows Antony's superiority over Brutus not only as a politician but as an orator of the first rank. He has learned how to move men by having kept company with them; he has learned from music the power of moving men through the use of verse; he has learned from plays the power of moving men through action and utterance, and he has learned from Caesar how to be ruthless and deceitful to achieve his purposes. At this point in the play, Antony clearly functions as a contrast to Brutus.

Antony's handling of the triumvirate is meant to contrast with Brutus' handling of the conspirators. Antony kills men freely when it suits his purpose; he compromises to maintain unity among his cohorts; he deceives and uses men to achieve his ends. His conduct of the triumvirate is immorally practical. Brutus, on the other hand, refuses to kill men who may harm his cause, refuses to make compromises to maintain unity, and refuses to deceive or use men to achieve his ends. His conduct of the conspiracy is moral and impractical, and it is through Antony's behavior that we learn how to judge Brutus' character.

Antony is used as a foil for Brutus for the last time in the play during the verbal battle which precedes his victory at Philippi. There Antony is shown at the peak of confidence, but Brutus is an equal match for him. Antony's courage and optimism in the face of battle is juxtaposed to Brutus' courage and pessimism in his anticipation of the decisive fight. Brutus' courage is made clear when he is seen as the equal opponent in the verbal duel and when his victory over Octavius is matched by Antony's over Cassius. Finally, Antony is made to deliver the eulogy over his enemy Brutus, so that the honor of Brutus becomes most emphatic when Antony admits, "This was the noblest Roman of them all."

Question: Who is the hero of *Julius Caesar*?

Answer: For centuries perplexed critics have wrestled with the question, who is the hero of the play? The tangled results of their considerations have left the question unanswered, or, at the most, with many answers. Let us then examine three suggestions among the many submitted. A) Caesar is the hero of the play. B) Brutus is the hero. C) Neither is the hero; the central interest of the play is its **theme** of rebellion.

A) Caesar may be regarded as the hero of the play not only because of the title or because historians have informed us of the profound interest Elizabethans had in the character of Caesar, or because there was a stage tradition of tyrant-kings who resembled Caesar, but because the play itself points to the fact that Caesar is its hero. The entire action of the play centers around Caesar's being, both corporeal and in spirit. The opening scene presents opposite views of Caesar, expressed by the tribunes, who hate him, and by the mob, which adores him. Subsequently, Caesar is seen marching in triumph, accompanied by pomp and pageantry which captivated the Elizabethan eye. (The audience paid rapt attention to tragedies of fallen monarchs of classical periods because of their resemblance to heroes of their own history, and they were accustomed to give first place in their minds to their own monarchs.) Caesar is the picture of a king, who, although seen infrequently, makes his presence felt continuously, and is the more honored because he is rarely seen.

Caesar's presence is next felt and visualized by Casca in his narrative of the events of the Lupercal. Next, Caesar is the center of Brutus' thoughts; what Caesar had been and what he may become is the problem which confronts the troubled patriot. Caesar is next seen in his domestic environment, then in the procession to the Senate. He is the focus of interest as Artemidorus petitions him and the Soothsayer warns him. All eyes are on Caesar when he opens the Senate on the fateful ides of March; his stature grows as his petitioners kneel before him. Overwhelmed by his self-importance, Caesar swells, reaches for the stars, falls. He is the target of the daggers in the hands of the outraged petitioners. And when the assassins step back, Caesar is dead center at the base of Pompey's statue.

After his assassination, his success and ambition are carried on in his image in the persons of Antony and Octavius, and his ghost visits his assassin seeking revenge. Finally, when the assassins die one by one, they die with the name Caesar on their lips. Thus, Caesar and the spirit of Caesar may be said to dominate the play, and the character of Caesar may be described as the tragic hero of the play.

B) If Brutus is to be called the hero of the play, the character of Caesar must be viewed in a different light. With Brutus as the hero, Caesar must be seen as pompous, arrogant, superstitious, infirm, overweening, and tyrannical. Brutus, the chief assassin, then can be seen as the hero, who out of duty to the Republic and in the spirit of freedom sacrifices his personal love for Caesar for the sake of the common good. He kills Caesar, whom he loves as a friend, because Caesar's ambitions endanger the freedom of all Romans. The tragedy of the noble Brutus becomes the tragedy of a man who was too true to his ideals to be good at the job of statecraft, which requires compromise. Brutus was too moral to execute the men who might harm him or to accept proposals which were tainted with self-interest or corruption. He was too noble to see that other men were not like himself, too eager to put his fate into the hands of the gods, whom he trusted. That Brutus was an honorable man was known by all men. Even Antony, an opportunist, who turned the mob against Brutus, knew that "this was the noblest Roman of them all."

C) If Shakespeare has written a problem play in which his principle concern is to examine the state of insurrection, the immorality of the act itself, and the evil which comes after, then *Julius Caesar* is play without a hero. It is a play of men who as individuals are both good and bad, men with mixed motives and mixed emotions, men with private as well as public needs, and men put to confusion by the disorder they have created. If the **theme** of rebellion is the central interest in the play, then Caesar is a courageous and heroic figure, who, inflated by success and weakened by age and physical and mental infirmities, forgets those who have helped him (both men and gods), and, through his outrageous arrogance in seeking the crown, tempts the gods and invites his own death at the hands of angry men.

Brutus, under these circumstances, is an insurgent, who, for just cause, does an immoral act and brings disaster to the Republic, which is greater than that which he had hoped to prevent. Caesar's rule, however despotic, must be seen as a unifying force in the Republic. He was destined to become king and found an empire. Brutus tried to interfere with destiny and slew Caesar, but, ironically, Caesar lived on. The spirit of Caesar or Caesarism survived the tyrant's death, and the empire, destined to be founded by "Caesar," was born under Octavius, who adopted the spirit and the name of Caesar.

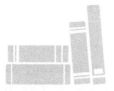

SUBJECT BIBLIOGRAPHY AND GUIDE TO RESEARCH PAPERS

The most important thing in the study of Shakespeare's plays is the selection of a suitable text. Most modern texts of *Julius Caesar* are based on the *First Folio* edition of his works (1623), which is a particularly good one and one of the few left intact when Shakespeare's texts were being altered and revised during the eighteenth and nineteenth centuries. There are numerous good editions of the play available in inexpensive bindings with notes, glossaries, and critical commentaries. The New American Library edition, the Folger Library edition, and the Bantam Classic Books edition are among the best. Students may prefer the Folger Library edition, which is printed in an attractive format with notes and pictures facing the text pages they explain. The reader wishing a more permanent edition might purchase the Arden Shakespeare. The most thorough and comprehensive version of the play is in the New Variorum edition of Shakespeare's Works. This work includes the complete text with all its variants as well as extensive excerpts from the sources and major critics, exhaustive textual notes, and an elaborate bibliography. The student will find in the Cambridge edition of the play, edited by W. A. Wright and W. G. Clark, the most authoritative text of the play. The Cambridge Shakespeare and a special version of it, published as the Globe edition, are generally regarded as the standard reading text for *Julius Caesar*.

Listed below is a selective bibliography of the more significant books and articles dealing generally with Shakespeare and his era, many of which contain references to the play. There are also listed more important critical analyses of the play itself. They are arranged alphabetically by author within key research topics.

CRITICISM AND INTERPRETATION OF JULIUS CAESAR

Ayres, H. "Shakespeare's *Julius Caesar* in the Light of Some Other Versions," *PMLA*, XXV (1910), 183-227.

Boas, F. S. *Shakespeare and his Predecessors. 1896.*

Bonjour, Adrien. *The Structure of Julius Caesar. 1958.*

Brooke, C. F. Tucker. *Shakespeare's Plutarch.* Vol. I: Containing the Main Sources of *Julius Caesar.* 1909.

Charney, Maurice. *Shakespeare's Roman Plays.* 1961.

Coleridge, Samuel Taylor. *Coleridge's Writing on Shakespeare*, ed. T. Hawkes, 1959.

Dean, Leonard F. *"Julius Caesar* and Modern Criticism," *The English Journal* (October 1961), 451-6.

Dennis, John. *On the Genius and Writings of Shakespeare. London, 1711. Reprinted in D. N. Smith, ed. Eighteenth-Century Essays on Shakespeare, 1903.*

Dorsh, T. S., ed. *Julius Caesar.* 1955.

Foakes, R. A. "An Approach to *Julius Caesar*," *Shakespeare Quarterly*, V (Summer, 1954), 259-70.

Hazlitt, William. *The Characters of Shakespeare's Plays. 1817.*

Hudson, Henry Norman. *Lectures on Shakespeare.* 1848.

Hunter, Sir Mark. *Transactions of the Royal Society of Literature. 1931.*

Kittredge, George Lyman, ed. *Julius Caesar.* 1939.

Knight, G. Wilson. *The Imperial **Theme**.* 1951.

MacCallum, M. W. *Shakespeare's Roman Plays and Their Background. 1910.*

Palmer, John. *Political Characters in Shakespeare. 1945.*

Phillips, James E., Jr. *The State in Shakespeare's Greek and Roman Plays. 1940.*

Schanzer, Ernest. "The Problem of *Julius Caesar*," *Shakespeare Quarterly*, VI (Summer, 1955), 297-308.

____. *The Problem Plays of Shakespeare. 1963.*

Smith, Gordon Ross. "Brutus, Virtue and Will," *Shakespeare Quarterly.* X (1959), 367-8.

Stirling, Brents. "Or Else This Were a Savage Spectacle," *PMLA*, LXVI (1951), 765-74.

____. *The Populace in Shakespeare. 1949.*